SEW UP A STORM:

All the Way to the Bank!

How to Succeed in a Sewing-Related Business

KAREN L. MASLOWSKI

This book was exhaustively researched to ensure accuracy and completeness of the information herein. The author assumes no responsibility for any inaccuracies, errors, omissions or inconsistencies represented in this book. Any slights to any people, places or organizations are completely unintentional.

Sew Up A Storm: All the Way to the Bank! Copyright © 1995 by Karen L. Maslowski. Printed and bound in the US.

All rights reserved.
No part of this book may be reproduced in any form or by any electronic or mechanical means without written permission by the publisher, except by a reviewer, who may quote brief passages to be printed in a magazine or newspaper.

For information, please contact:

SewStorm Publishing
944 Sutton Road
Cincinnati, OH 45230-3581.

ISBN 0-9648729-1-9

Library of Congress Catalog Card Number: 95-92592

Cover design by Barbara M. Libby

TABLE OF CONTENTS

PART THREE:

PARAPHERNALIA

PART FOUR:

RELATED FIELDS

PART FIVE:

SUMMARY & INCOME INFO

PART SIX:

REFERENCE SECTION

PART SEVEN:

BIBLIOGRAPHY

INDEX

ACKNOWLEDGMENTS

Many people gave support to this project. To anyone I've inadvertently left out: you are not forgotten, and your help was greatly appreciated.

I am indebted to the entire Professional Sewing Association, but especially to Deborah Jackson, Barbara Shelton, Dawn Haugom, and Mary Kay DeBruler, for their encouragement and cheerleading. Thanks to Reneé Morgenstern for urging me to write the book in the first place, and for handing over a wonderful legacy in the PSA newsletter. Joyce Smith of Ohio State University Extension deserves an extra big thanks for helping me develop the survey that got the ball rolling, as does Karen Howland for the initial idea of a fact-gathering vehicle and what questions should be included. Karen's unflagging enthusiasm through the years it took to get to this point, and our many hours of phone conversations reminded me why I was writing this book. Much love and gratitude go to Claire Shaeffer, who did her best to help me get this work published, and encouraged me all the way to the end.

I'm grateful to all the PACC, PSA and PNG members and others who responded to my survey. All those who were interviewed are appreciated most heartily, especially the ones who wrote periodically to keep me abreast of changes in their businesses. I deeply appreciate the time taken to fill out the survey and to talk with me. A special thanks to the other business owners who allowed me to interview them, also. Without you, there would be no book, and I thank you.

For their kind, helpful editorial advice (some of it very humbling), thank you: Karen Howland, Kateri Ellison, and Edie Cooper. Barbara Libby is appreciated for her elegant cover design and advice. Also, thanks to my husband, Steve Maslowski, who did a yeoman, 11th hour job of cleaning up and polishing the manuscript. It made all the difference in readability.

My entire family deserves praise for their forbearance and patience with me as I devoted my time to what must have seemed to them my fourth, most demanding child. My daughters are especially appreciated: to Christy, for her unflagging support and belief in me, and to Robin and Holly for allowing me to work when I had to. The book is dedicated to my three girls, with love.

As a former boss used to tell me, "You can never say 'thank you' too many times." So again, many thanks to everyone.

Karen L. Maslowski, August 18, 1995

INTRODUCTION

If you're about to read this book, you are probably interested in turning your sewing interests and talents into a profitable venture, a business of some kind. *Sew Up A Storm: All the Way to the Bank!* was written as a reference for you, as a shortcut to the process I went through several years ago.

In 1988, I asked a close friend how her husband liked his technically oriented job as a financial advisor for institutional traders. Her answer gave me pause: "Woody's lucky; his vocation is also his avocation. He would rather do this than anything else."

My husband has similar job satisfaction in his career as a wildlife photographer. Sure, parts of it are challenging, but given a choice, Steve would rather be taking pictures than doing almost anything else. Reflecting on my own occupation of selling insurance, I realized this was not the case with me. There were many times when the prospect of yet another fifty-hour week of trying to persuade people to spend major dollars on a product they couldn't see, touch, or impress their friends with was just too daunting. My creativity was stifled, too.

This dissatisfaction stayed with me, until finally I felt I could no longer handle the high stress of insurance sales. I found I really wanted to incorporate sewing into a profit-making venture. A lifelong passion, sewing seemed to be the ticket to my own brand of career fulfillment.

My first steps to realizing this goal began with membership in the Greater Cincinnati Professional Sewing Association (PSA). Here I found others like me – people who had left teaching careers, sales positions, and engineering jobs for more satisfying work in a sewing business. For so long there had been no one to talk with about my hopes, fears and aspirations; I felt as if I had come out of the closet with my sewing obsession.

Since I was still trying to find my own niche in sewing, my time at monthly meetings was spent pumping other members for information. By chance, a few months after I joined the Cincinnati organization the newsletter editor asked for a replacement. I volunteered. I soon initiated a new regular feature in the monthly newsletter, a "Member Profile" column, which gave me a chance to get to know the other sewing professionals and learn about the pros and cons of their respective specialties.

Along the way some interesting facts emerged: First, sewing is a very diverse business. It was intriguing to see how each sewing pro had taken her special interests and made a profitable venture of it. However, no two businesses were alike. Second, I discovered I loved to write, especially about sewing, and most particularly about sewing as a business. I also realized I wanted to teach others to sew, rather than sewing for others. Third, it had become clear to me that after a lifetime of being a nearly perfect pattern size (too bad that's no longer true), I did not have the experience in alterations necessary for a successful dressmaking career. Making the same item over and over again didn't appeal to me, either.

One hitch in my information gathering process was that I couldn't find any data about earnings' potential in sewing. This was unbelievable: how could I choose my business specialty when I had no clear idea of the monetary rewards? I wanted to know how much sewing pros were making, and the books written about sewing businesses didn't address this issue to my satisfaction. They also glossed over the possibility of any kind of business other than dressmaking. Moreover, the only books I knew about were written in the previous few years: How did the businesses that were already in existence even get started without any guidelines or support? It was obvious that these entrepreneurs were pathfinding – making the rules and creating their own opportunities as they went along.

No one had ever carefully studied the realities of the sewing-related industry. With the advent of the Professional Association of Custom Clothiers (PACC), dressmaking, in particular, was suddenly being promoted by *Sew News* and other national publications as a viable career option. However, many other specialties are virtually invisible as possible industries. For example, when was the last time you saw a study of grinding machine cover manufacturers? You probably never have, because many of them are cottage industries, just as so many other sewing-related enterprises are.

To get a feel for what was being done around the country, I listed the sewn products in a current Lillian Vernon mail order catalogue. The list was three pages long. Next, I browsed my local Yellow Pages and wrote down the headings that applied to sewing. This yielded another three pages. Curiously, only four of the forty local Professional Sewing Association, Inc. (PSA) members, all with legitimate businesses, were listed under any of these topics. How were they so successful without advertising in this most traditional way?

A conversation with fellow PSA member Karen Howland led to the refinement of a survey for sewing professionals that I decided to test among our local membership. Four pages of questions served to gather information that I hoped would show some sort of pattern. Including in the survey was a question dealing with hourly income. To my absolute delight (and shock), most of the members responded to the survey and even answered the query about income.

The idea to write a book on this topic had been brewing in my mind for quite some time. The only hindrance to an interesting account was my limited knowledge of what was being done in sewing in other parts of the country, not just in the Cincinnati area. The idea light went on when I found that I could buy the mailing labels for the 700 PACC members across the country. Eureka! Joyce Smith, the Clothing and Textile specialist of the Ohio State University Extension, helped streamline the survey. I then mailed it to over 500 members, in addition to nearly 100 sewing pros I found on the Internet.

My research indicated that a good survey usually yields about a 5-10% return; after only three months, I had received replies of nearly 40% of them, with more coming in daily. These people were eager to share their experiences!

The following text tells the stories of many of these sewing professionals and others. They are serious business people who just happen to be making money doing what they love, in a utilitarian, creative, and/or artistic field. Many of the businesses discussed are small one-person operations, and many of the subjects are self-employed, and often home-based. Also included are profiles of businesses that have grown beyond their creators' wildest dreams.

Possible earnings' ranges are discussed wherever the data was available. But the operative maxim is "you can get out of this business whatever you are willing to put into it." Whether you choose to spend a few hours a month, or 12 hours a day, it's at the option of the individual; many of the options discussed are still cottage industries. Many of the people interviewed began their businesses in a corner of their homes. When their business imposed on their living space, they branched out further. Some merely took over a bigger portion of the home; still others have gone on to retail storefront spaces and beyond, as you will see.

If you have ever dreamed of turning your sewing talents into making money for a rainy day or have wanted to know how you can make a living (and how much you can make) by sewing, this book will enlighten you and encourage you to act upon your desires. Gone forever is the quaint image of the grey-bunned elderly woman who "takes in sewing", starving in the process.

Sew up a storm! All the way to the bank.

Part One:

Clothing

↳ **Custom Dressmaking, Patternmaking, Couture Sewing**

↳ **Alterations, Restyling, Concierge Services**

↳ **Custom Design: Square Dance/Western Wear, Clothing for Special Needs**

↳ **Bridal & Formalwear**

↳ **Lingerie to Outerwear**

↳ **Custom Tailoring, Menswear, Shirtmaking, Uniforms**

↳ **Furs & Leathers: Faux & Genuine**

↳ **Costumes: Theatric, Fantastic & Exotic**

↳ **Kid Stuff: Children's Clothing**

Chapter 1

Custom Dressmaking, Patternmaking, Couture Sewing

Dressmaking

The human form stubbornly defies description as a shape; it is not easily defined as a cylinder or a cube because of the infinite variations in its planes and curves. This is especially true of the female body. The necessity of this form to move adds another dimension to designing clothing for it. A good custom dressmaker takes endless variables into account to design a garment with a fit that is impossible to imitate with mass-produced methods.

Dressmaking is the custom manufacture of clothing not strictly tailored, including dresses, pants, blouses, skirts and other garments for women. Fitting to the customer's measurements makes the difference between a custom garment and one "off the rack". Fees for these services can range from low to astronomical depending on the skill of the dressmaker, designs implemented, the patterns being used or created, and the economic climate of the region.

In 1906, 7 ½ pages of the Cincinnati city directory listed over 1,100 dressmakers (there were 14 pages of saloons!). Add to that figure nearly 600 tailors and 150 millinery establishments, and you had quite a number of nimble fingers flying over fabric in a population of approximately 350,000 . In the early 1980's the area had grown to over 1½ million people, yet there were only nine dressmakers, no milliners, and only ten tailors. Of course, the numbers of retail stores near the turn of the century were limited, which is certainly not true today.

This recent proliferation of retail stores, with their almost overwhelming choice of the same garment repeated in endless colors and fabrications, has turned out to be both a blessing and a curse for the professional dressmaker. The customer, familiar with dressing exactly like her peers and wearing the "latest" look, often does not realize how poorly her ready-made clothing fits.

Sometimes the customer thinks having something made will save money over buying a ready-made garment. Most of the clothing for sale today in the US is quickly made with cheap overseas labor in mass lots. Thus, it can be sold for a very low price.

How can a dressmaker compete with these low prices and poor construction? She shouldn't. When a dressmaker creates a garment for a client, it cannot possibly compare in price to its mass-produced counterpart sold in a store. Patterns, fabrics, and trims are all chosen in a unique combination and sewn to fit one particular body, as opposed to the mythical "size 10" of the apparel manufacturers. One dressmaker told me that she had created her own problem with her customers' perceptions in this regard. "I'd been accepting compliments on my own clothes by replying that I'd made them myself – and it only cost me $5.00! This was a big mistake. It gave people the impression that me sewing for them would save *them* money, too; I hadn't taken into consideration the time I spent looking for fabric, let alone the time it took to sew! I now realize my time is worth more than I thought."

Educate Your Customer

A dressmaker must be able to educate her customer; educate her with regard to quality of workmanship, fabric, design and fit. A client may ask to have something made that is not flattering to her figure or coloring, or the fabric chosen may be ill-suited to the project. Diplomacy and the ability to know whether to bite your tongue or to say "this is a better length for you, Mrs. Jones", are truly necessary attributes. The psychology of fit should also be carefully studied by professional dressmakers. Ohio dressmaker and bridal designer **Karen Howland** says: "Listen with your eyes. Watch the client's hands for clues to what she is *really* saying. Whatever her hands keep going to is what she is most worried about, even if she *says* it's fine." Often it's necessary to take control of the situation, and ask leading questions, eliciting the customer's true feelings. (See Chapter 4 for more on Bridal.)

Machines

Howland also has this advice for prospective dressmakers: don't wait until you can afford the fanciest equipment. Even though some of the newer machines have all the bells and whistles, you probably can get by with a domestic zigzag machine and a good iron for a while. Once you begin to make money, Karen suggests investing in a commercial machine and/or serger. Commercial tailoring/dressmaking machines sew at least three times faster than domestic models, allowing you to maximize use of your sewing time.

If your customers like the look of a machine hem, invest in a blindstitch machine for speedy hemming. Howland agonized over her decision to spend what felt like too much money at the time when she bought her Babylock hemmer, but it quickly paid for itself. She charges one price for a hand hem, and a lower price for a machine hem. This pricing fairly compensates her based on the actual use of her time. It also alerts the customer to the extra time and care taken in a hand hem. A wise investment might be a professional quality pressing system, like a gravity feed iron.

Buying Fabric

Another important consideration for dressmakers concerns the purchase of fabric. Buying at retail prices makes it virtually impossible to markup fabric used in customer's goods. However, buying raw materials wholesale and adding a percentage onto the sales price can significantly increase your profits. Traditionally, other types of service businesses buy wholesale, then sell retail. Auto repair shops, furnace technicians, and remodelers all buy their parts and materials at a professional discount, the mark them up. It helps cover their time devoted to purchasing and maintaining inventory. Sometimes the markup may be 30-50%.

Buying wholesale can be a problem for many, especially those just starting out in business. Karen Howland recommends making your first contact with a wholesaler sound as if you do this every day; do not be timid, or you will not be taken seriously. When you are ready to find wholesale sources for fabric, notions and findings such as thread, buttons, interfacings, and machine supplies, a good place to start is in the Thomas Register, available in most public libraries. Also check with your librarian to find listings of trade periodicals by area of specialty. Many sources advertise in these magazines and newsletters. There are also numerous regional shows where hundreds of companies are represented. Attending one of these shows will help you find what you are looking for. If you do not find exactly what you need, company representatives may know where to find the item, and it pays to develop a continuing business relationship with them. (See Chapter 14 for a more in-depth discussion of attending shows.) Some companies have a swatch service, which makes choosing fabrics easier for your client, too. (For more info on buying fabrics, see Chapter 23.)

Be Business-like

Be sure you are in business to make a profit, not just as a hobby. Comply with all the Federal, state and local legal and tax regulations that apply to your type of business, including the collection and remittance of applicable sales taxes. Establish a major credit card account and use it for your business purchases. Open a checking account just for business receipts and expenditures, and never commingle your personal transactions in this account.

Commercial Patterns

Pattern use can also be a sticky issue. Dressmakers have traditionally taken the use of commercial patterns for granted. Generally speaking, using a commercial pattern to make individually fitted garments is allowed. However, wholesale duplication of a commercial pattern is not legal because of copyrights owned by the pattern publishers. Be alert to this potentially serious violation.

Karen Howland and **Juliene Goins** of North Carolina use their own patternmaking techniques from the customer's measurements; other dressmakers use a variety of patterns such as commercial, computer generated, and a combination of these methods. **Joanne Kristopik** of Connecticut uses the Dress Shop computer software to augment and fine tune her patterns, often combining them with parts of a Vogue, Butterick, or other commercial method. Joanne occasionally makes muslins of her designs, at an additional cost to the customer.

Kateri Ellison of Washington, DC says: "Like the little old dressmaker of days gone by, I make my own patterns." But unlike that dusty old image, Kateri uses patternmaking software to generate slopers and to draft her own patterns. Clients often ask her to copy designer garments from pictures or sketches, and she also "cannibalizes" parts from commercial patterns.

Ellison's exposure to the dressmaking business started early in her childhood. Her great aunt had a successful dressmaking business in New Orleans, billing herself as "Modeste the Modiste". An aunt also took in sewing. Like many, Ellison often stayed up late on Saturday nights making a new dress for Sunday Mass. Her mother wouldn't let her stint on quality, and would make Kateri rip out any subpar stitching. Her mother was also responsible for the purchase of some pre-World War II sewing books that Ellison credits with the foundation of her sewing knowledge. "I sew the old, traditional way, though the construction techniques in patterns today are easier."

Ellison's career in sewing waited in the wings for many years while she held several government jobs. Sixteen years in the Department of Defense were followed by five years with the Bureau of Indian Affairs. After another seven years of service in Washington, DC government as a Chief Administrative Officer in the Consumer and Regulatory Affairs Department, Kateri decided to leave government life and open a full-time sewing business. She had received many inquiries from co-workers and projected that she would have a ready-made customer base, which has turned out to be the case. In early 1991, she sent out invitations and flyers to 100 people on her initial contacts' list. A whopping 30% response started her up and running right away. This base has expanded regularly by referrals from pleased customers.

Her townhouse is 1½ miles from the White House, and Kateri sees clients in a consultation area carved out of the living room, where she has fabric samples on display from various sources. Kateri measures customers upstairs, where she conducts all other sewing business, in one of the two huge master bedroom suites modified to be more business-like for this purpose.

For security's sake, her business card only details her business name, business hours, and phone number, with no address. She utilizes a voice mail system that allows her to segregate business calls from personal calls to her and her husband, maintaining a professional profile, even on the phone.

A recent episode reminded Kateri that keeping a professional image is vitally important. While shopping at Nieman Marcus, she mentioned to the sales clerk that she was a dressmaker. Since the store has had trouble finding enough competent people to handle their volume of alterations, Ellison was asked to send her price list to the store. Its professional appearance surprised the clerk, who apparently hadn't expected anything quite so organized from a dressmaker.

Despite the competitive atmosphere in the Capitol, Ellison reports that her business is flourishing. She has accepted some unusual assignments, but prefers to create and sew designer-quality clothing. One job consisted of making 22 identical suits for a club. "I will never do that again. It didn't get any faster with repetition because it was so boring."

Storefront Businesses

Mary Bahl works from her home in Omaha. A street level, walk-out basement is her studio, segregating her work totally from her the rest of the house. Downsizing at her former place of employment offered Mary the opportunity to take early retirement. She decided to open her own sewing business by building on her 30 years sewing experience and her training from the Ann Hyde School in Colorado, where she had twice attended sessions. Omaha lacked what Mary considered "a real good fabric store", so her original plans were to open her own. A consultation with a SCORE (Service Corps of Retired Executives) volunteer convinced her not to, because the time and requirement of such a venture were more than she was willing to commit to. As an alternative, Mary decided to sew for others. Her current home was chosen with this goal in mind. She and her husband moved there shortly after she retired, and she immediately opened for business in December of 1991.

Like Kateri Ellison, Bahl had clientele right from the start. For years, she had been sewing part time for people in her office. Though she'd never anticipated sewing for money, her company forced her to rethink her career path. Now she really enjoys it. "Sometimes I get frustrated, but somehow, things work out." She finds the work rewarding, especially the frequent praise from customers and the feeling of accomplishment. Her former job had been all computer work with little job satisfaction.

Bahl feels that the advantages of having her business in her home outweigh the disadvantages. She can work when she wants to; she keeps a 9 to 5 schedule, but if she has something else to do, she does it. For instance, when her mother-in-law died, Mary was free to deal with the details of settling the estate. "Being your own person and setting your own goals is better than being an employee. Having clients and commitments is not the same as having to report to someone else." Mary concludes the only real drawback of her business is the isolation of working alone, particularly after years of working for a big company. To combat loneliness, she tries to have lunch out with another homebased seamstress once a week.

Some clients think they can drop in on her anytime, but Mary tries to maintain regular store hours. To completely ensure clients don't invade your privacy, a separate shop is the only answer.

Juliene Goins decided to move her business to a separate location after 12 years of sewing from her home. In a storefront in Pinehurst, the "Golf Capitol of North Carolina", Goins found the ideal spot for her custom sewing business. The former restaurant site is beside a highway, with a busy shopping center nearby, creating a large volume of drive-by traffic. A nice display area in the front of the shop features Juliene's custom-made accessories (see Chapter 14). In the back are the workroom and a dressing area outfitted with two mirrors, and a stool for customers to stand on while garments are measured for hems.

Courses at nearby Southern Pines Community College taught Juliene tailoring, hat-making and pattern design, and gave her freedom from the constraints imposed by commercial patterns. Using the customer's measurements, Goins drafts a pattern and adds design details. She believes her customers appreciate this more couture approach to sewing, along with the hand hems and the other fine handwork that she does. One particularly fussy customer taught her a lesson by insisting that Juliene redo a garment four times before it was acceptable. Since that experience, she makes sure she does the work right the first time!

After several similar incidents, and situations where the client wanted jobs finished early, Juliene initiated a policy of drafting contracts for all her jobs. She developed a standard 3-part form for this purpose. The customer has a three day recission period from the date of signing to cancel the contract. After that, the contract stands and the customer must pay to get the fabric back. If the article is not picked up in 30 days after the customer has been notified of its completion, Goins sells the garment to defray her costs. She also charges a $35 measuring fee for new customers and credits this charge against the final bill. "Just like the lawyers do," she says. Unless an existing customer changes the original contract, she does not charge for a measuring and consultation appointment.

Other dressmakers suggest asking for a deposit up front. One says "I'm not embarrassed to ask for a deposit; if they do not want to pay it, especially on detailed or expensive designs, then I feel they will renege on the contract anyway, and I don't want them as a customer." The consensus is the more you charge, the better clientele you will have. "Use good fabric, do an exceptional job for the client, add extras (like personalized labels), and they will continue to do business with you." One seamstress refused to put her label in some garments because the client insisted on using an inadvisable combination of fabrics – with disastrous results.

Juliene Goins uses another form that she adapted from Mary Roehr's book, *Sewing as a Home Business.* A task sheet is attached to every job accepted, documenting all the customer's requirements. Juliene says that this eliminates arguments with the customer by providing a written record of all the tasks performed. Dorothy Moore's *Pattern Drafting and Dressmaking* was the source for the two measurement charts Juliene uses. She added a space for her customers' names at the bottom, which is filled in and attached to the task sheet. One of these forms is for dress measurements, the other for pants. Both of these go into a work-in-progress folder until the tasks are completed, then filed permanently for future reference.

For hourly work, Juliene uses a time chart also adapted from Mary Roehr's book. Goins times herself for each task's stop and start time. In this way, she can keep better track of what is taking the most time, and where she can become more efficient.

Because other business people wouldn't share information with her, Goins "learned to look and observe". She found wholesale sources on her own, refusing to pay retail for items like fixtures, display cases, mannequins, tailoring tickets, garment bags, and packaging supplies.

Pricing

Many dressmakers have trouble setting their price structure to provide enough profit. **Karen Watson** of Virginia (profiled in Chapter 15) says "even though my Master's thesis was on pricing, I still struggle with this issue." Since she is the sole breadwinner of her family, pricing is especially critical for her. Sewing allows her to stay home with her husband who has health problems. Luckily, business has been good. "I never lack for business; I always have a backlog of 20 or so projects," she says. Watson wants to increase her output through expansion, but she has a hard time finding qualified help, despite the heavy demand for her sewing services.

Nancy Marden (profiled in Chapter 24), has this to say about pricing her dressmaking services: "Price is vital; if you price yourself out of the market, you won't have any business, especially in an area of poor economy, like where I live in the Northeast." Nancy had to make a choice between charging more and having repeat business; she chose the latter, hoping her average hourly income would go up. Sewing for the same people would increase her efficiency, due to the ease of fitting a body she is already familiar with and the familiarity of "selling" them. One of the hardest things about working with customers is getting them used to paying a dressmaker.

Marden says she is getting better at saying "This is a ballpark figure" to her clients, letting them know that there can be additional costs due to conditions not readily apparent during the initial consultation. Aware that many dressmakers want to professionalize in the eyes of the public, she feels that some of their elitist attitude is ill-placed. She questions whether the skill level is equal to that of a physician or a dentist, and estimates it is probably closer to that of an auto mechanic, or a hairdresser. "We have come to rely on their services, and we have adapted to their schedules. The same cannot yet be said of custom sewing" in many areas of the country. Being available to serve her customers' needs is part of the service she feels she needs to offer them.

Patternmaking

"I've 'microwaved' pattern fitting for home sewers, dressmakers and tailors," says **Gayle Taylor**. This Texan has revolutionized the use of commercial patterns. On a per use fee basis, Gayle and her staff, with the aid of over 75 measurements supplied by the customer, will custom fit any pattern to the customer's precise body shape. "Accurate measurements lead to accurate fit," says Taylor.

During her twenty years of dressmaking experience, Taylor says fitting was a perennial problem. She finally stopped her other daily activities to research and analyze "fit". She began by measuring patterns, then comparing body measurements. This led to the development of a pair of tools to set up "anchoring points" on the body. The system she developed uses metric measurements for greater accuracy. "It's all math and geometry," Gayle says.

According to Taylor, during the seventies and early eighties pattern companies misread the decline in home sewing. She believes they never addressed the fitting issue, at a time when the age and weight ranges of their customers moved up the scale. Though Gayle doesn't exclusively target the home sewing market, she does draw from that group, as well as from dressmakers and tailors. Her service allows a cut, sew and wear approach to sewing a commercial pattern with a guaranteed fit.

Gayle Taylor Clothes That Fit, Inc. takes patterns sent to them, together with the 75+ measurements, then redraws the pattern on new tissue and glassine paper, using Gayle's unique method. Her "Cut to Fit...perfectly!" pattern adjustment service carries fees ranging from $30 for a straight or A-line skirt, to $75 for a wedding dress. If the customer prefers, the "Made to Fit...perfectly!" side of the business will create the garment using the client's own pattern and fabric at fees ranging from $75 for an unlined skirt, to $220 for an unlined, princess seamed dress with sleeves. This service carries a stated turnaround time of 18 days or less.

Other services offered by Taylor include a Personal Fit Profile for the customer, identifying "style lines" that flattering that person, and those that don't, with recommended current pattern numbers. Her customers receive seasonal newsletters to help them stay current with fashion directions. Several fabric stores around the country now offer a measuring option as a prelude to using the "Cut to Fit...perfectly!" service.

Couture Sewing

In the airy stratosphere of couture sewing, there are relatively few who can command the prices and the clientele of the big design houses. One who has managed to do this quite well is **Kenneth D. King**, a noted San Francisco designer. Making his reputation through a line of accessories (see Chapter 13 for more of Kenneth's amazing story), King branched out into more custom fitted clothing. His well-heeled and high profile clients were asking him to expand on the magnificent heavily embellished vests he'd been creating, so he began making one-of-a-kind garments on a commission basis. Although King "used to feel inferior about not having an art background," his creativity is one of his biggest strengths.

Fitting Issues

With his hats and vests, "fit" was not an issue, and when he found the demand for his clothing so high, Kenneth looked around for someone to teach him the definitive fitting method, especially for his strapless garments. Finally, in 1990, he found a patternmaker who had trained at the Chambres Syndicale in Paris. She taught him the French art of "moulage", a method of creating a sloper directly from the measurements of the person for whom the garment is being made. With this new knowledge, King says his ability to fit the figure took a "quantum leap". "No other way worked; with this method I found out why it works, and I can draft a pattern, put it right into the fashion fabric if I want to, and have it fit."

Moulage involves taking the client's measurements, and applying geometry to come up with a skin-tight sloper that exactly corresponds to body shape. "Some of the slopers look like something out of Dr. Suess when they're finished, but that's what their bodies are really like, though they may not seem that way in real life."

Using this system allows King to limit the number of fittings he requires, which is good for both him and his high-profile clientele. Kenneth feels that lazy habits on the part of clothing manufacturers, and "benign neglect" in clothing design, beginning in the late sixties led to a confusion on the part of the consumer about what constitutes good fit. "If you do not educate people as to fit in their clothing, they won't know to demand it. Stretch fabrics can be fudged by manufacturers."

With a background in both marketing and retailing, King feels he has an edge over some designers. He's sensitive to demand; in retailing you can't just throw something out on the sales floor and expect it to sell. The product has to fulfill a need. Kenneth keeps his finger on the pulse of what his clients will want. His retailing experience also showed him the wisdom of having a nice studio – customers are willing to pay higher prices when their surroundings are more luxurious. King's studio includes a waiting room decked out with some of his gorgeous furniture pieces, covered in rich velvets and embellished with the beading and other touches he is famous for. Some of Kenneth's unusual clocks adorn the area, as well.

Paying the Bills

King also keeps his eye on the bottom line. He pays his bills on time, and expects the same from his customers. In fact, he only sends retail shipments C.O.D., a practice virtually unheard of. In retail, most vendors are carried on account. "You don't have to go the established route in business," King says. He also cautions that "you'd better have a product that justifies an unorthodox business practice."

Stanley Marcus, of the famed Nieman-Marcus store chain, said of Kenneth King: "There is a small audience for his work, but when he unearths them, he will do very well." He has dug them up, and is doing quite well, thank you.

Museum Quality

The curator at the Los Angeles County Museum of Art visited Kenneth's studio to view his current work. Upon seeing the various garments, furniture, jewelry, hats and clockwork fantasies, the curator urged King to think as a historian. He believed that Kenneth's creations would someday be sought after by museums for their costume collections, and suggested King keep track of pieces that he sold. The curator told him "We are interested in your work whenever you or your customers are ready to part with them." Some of Kenneth's work has already found a home there, including a magnificent strapless, form-fitting, pleated "mermaid" dress, with lettuce-edged ruffles at the hem and fantastic "leaves" forming the bodice. King is known for his strapless garments that "a woman can put on, wear, and not think about," because they are so well constructed they stay put.

Teaching at the Sewing Workshop in San Francisco allows Kenneth to broaden his scope of activities and has led to a starring role in a PBS television series co-sponsored by Vogue and Bernina. Hosted by Nancy Fleming, the former Miss America who won the talent competition with her sewing talents, the series "sets the standard for all other sewing shows," according to King. Interviews with designers such as Bill Blass and Todd Oldham spice up the series, along with King's enthusiastic segments on beading, fitting and other "gourmet" techniques.

Asked if he had any words of wisdom for others in a sewing business, King said "You have to be willing, as I was, to sleep on the studio sofa, if you have to, listening to the mousetraps clack like castanets all night. Stick with it, and eventually you will get there. So many don't stick with it, and they fail. But, boy, does it feel good when it takes off! It's worth it." On whether he wears anything from his own collection (as Al Pacino, Elton John and other notables do), King, with characteristic aplomb, says "I've made my statement by making the pieces; others make theirs by wearing them."

Chapter 2

Alterations, Restyling, Concierge Services

Even though ready-to-wear clothing can be expensive, it often doesn't fit well. Most of today's retail clothing is manufactured overseas with cheap labor and low quality fabrics, and is inferior to items sold fifteen or twenty years ago. Off-the-rack clothing often requires the additional expense of alterations to get the right fit. Also, people keep their better clothes longer, maintaining them in a state of good repair, and adjusting them for this year's length or width. For the experienced sewing professional, there is a wealth of business in alterations.

Home Business

When a friend with an alterations' shop asked **Joy Lockwood** to help her during one busy Christmas season, it launched Joy's sewing business into a new and different direction. She was sewing for others, but when buying clothes for herself, she frequently passed on otherwise attractive garments that didn't fit perfectly. She had never thought about altering them, until working for her friend. "I learned a lot about alterations," she says. "I also learned how to handle customers. My employer had a smooth way with people." From this experience she learned there was a market for alterations and realized the potential to make much more money in this area than from dressmaking.

While Lockwood still does dressmaking for bridal and formal occasions, the alterations business has spilled over into this area, too. One of her customers, a bridesmaid 6 or 7 times, was planning a cruise and asked Joy to restyle a few of her old dresses. Imagine the range of alterations' sales that could be generated from the range of bodies represented in just one wedding.

Lockwood operates her business from her family's roomy 4-bedroom ranch home, where she uses about half of the basement. A 4' by 8' cutting table with a rotary mat to fit, gravity-feed iron and a vacuum ironing board are integral tools in Joy's business. The iron and table were big investments, but they make a big difference in the finished product. Her fitting area is located on the first floor of her home, and is equipped with a consultation area with a desk and two chairs, and mirrored closet doors. A fitting platform that allows Lockwood easier access to hems of long garments. This arrangement makes it convenient for Joy to temporarily leave work-in-progress when greeting and meeting with clients.

Alterations Shop

While Joy only gradually became aware of the possibilities of alterations as a business, **Mary Kay DeBruler** had always wanted to open a shop exclusively for alterations. She was working as an assistant to an oral surgeon, but attended tailoring classes in her spare time, with the hope of someday opening her own business. Shortly before the doctor retired, Mary Kay left to work in the alterations' department of a bridal shop. Next she move to an upscale dress shop, and finally to a Sak's Fifth Avenue store that opened in her area.

During this whole time, Mary Kay was also doing alterations for her local dry cleaners. They eventually suggested she rent a space adjacent to their shop for her business. Although DeBruler was not actively looking for a shop, she decided it was time to venture out on her own. "I had to go for it," she says. It turned out to be a good move. Her Nu-Look Alterations shop, while not affiliated with the Nu-Look Cleaners next door, has benefited greatly from being in the same building. They refer business to her, and allow her to attach flyers to cleaning that is being picked up. "I highly recommend this kind of arrangement to anyone; see what you can work out with a cleaner. This way you do your own thing, but have them as a backup" she says. "I love it."

Concentrating only on alterations, Mary Kay feels that she is making more income than with custom sewing. Though custom work is her strong suit, she makes less on it because it is more time-consuming than alterations. Her experience at Saks provided "an educational challenge", since she was working on more complicated garments. Taking apart garments made by others and figuring out how they are constructed is an interesting part of the job. DeBruler says "if someone put it together it can't be too tough to figure out even the most complex article of clothing. It keeps me interested in what I'm doing."

Nancy Marden does dressmaking and alterations, and teaches sewing in a small town in Maine. Surprisingly, she has a full-time job, too! (See Chapter 24). She does all the alterations for the local dry cleaner, which accounts for about 2/3 of her alterations' business. She also gets referrals from a nearby fabric store. She has developed a regular clientele of a substantial size. Recently, Nancy did over 600 alterations in one six month period.

You might say that **Gay Costa**'s career began at the same time the Professional Sewing Association started in Cincinnati. In 1985, she attended the original organizational meeting which persuaded her to adopt a more serious attitude about her sewing, an avocation since high school. Like Joy Lockwood, Costa also started her professional alterations' career under the tutelage of a fellow PSA member and shop owner.

Gay worked at a bridal shop for a time, where she learned to alter more complicated garments. It was after this experience that she decided to work full-time in alterations and dressmaking. With a feeling she ought to have a regular income, she soon went "back to work", managing Bonwit Teller's alterations shop, even though she had developed relationships with several dry cleaners and dress shops. She later changed her family situation and revived her business. Fortunately, she was able to regain all her former clients. Her former job at Bonwit's provided contacts leading to even more regular customers.

Costa resumed her self employment out of her basement, but soon outgrew that space. She remodeled the garage in her home and created a beautiful, light-filled workspace for her and two employees: her mother and daughter. A year later, she needed even more space, so she rented a 1,000 square foot storefront right in front of a drive-through bank window. The bank traffic soon provided a steady stream of customers into the shop. Business flourished to the point that Gay abandoned dressmaking to concentrate on alterations. She now has two full-time employees. The move to "the street" turned out to be a good one.

Deanna Witsken took a job in the alterations' department of a major department store after graduating from high school. She spent a portion of her three years there in the tailoring department, where being a woman, she was definitely in the minority. Until then, all the store's tailoring had been done exclusively by men. She says she "picked their brains, while they pinched my buns," and she learned all she could about tailoring. After marrying, she went to work at another department store as half of a two-woman alterations department. This was a great opportunity for Deanna to broaden her skills because this department did all the store's tailoring too.

When she started a family, Witsken decided that she never wanted to work for anyone else again. Dressmaking out of her home was not much of a challenge, but her kids did end up with fantastic clothing. So fantastic, she began to get a steady stream of business making children's apparel. Selling her creations at arts and craft shows kept Deanna busy for a while. Then disaster struck. Her son John was hit by a car, severely injured, and needed 24-hour care from Deanna for the next year.

After her son learned to walk again, Deanna was eager for something to do. Drawing from an inventory of her craft creations and children's items, she began selling items through a consignment shop. When she started making more money than the person who owned the shop, she decided to open her own business together with a sewing friend. Soon she bought her partner out and the focus of the shop changed to alterations and custom design.

Like many of the people interviewed for this book, Witsken did not have good luck with the SCORE advice that she received from the Small Business Administration when she sought advice from them. "They wanted to tell me how to mark hems; that was not one of my questions," she says. "They don't relate well to women in business. My most useful business information came from listening to Bruce Williams' daily radio talk show program, Talk Net.

In four years, Deanna's Designs had grown to include office space in two locations in the same building. Feeling disorganized, and seriously concerned by the unpleasant metamorphosis of the shoe store next door into a rowdy neighborhood bar, she searched for another location. She moved a half block away from her original location to a 1,400 square foot storefront, where she employs an enlarged staff of four full-time and two part-time employees. A sales area in the front of the shop showcases garments made during slow seasons, bolts of fabric, and original accessory items.

Now that Witsken has been in these quarters for several years, she says "My business has gone full circle. I began by offering lots of services, then I narrowed my focus, and now I'm expanding it again." While alterations was once the mainstay of her business, she has shifted back to doing more custom sewing. In 1993 Witsken hired an alterations' manager thus allowing Deanna the freedom to do what she wants to do: concentrate on design. "After seven years in this business, people are coming in for one of a kind designs, and are willing to pay for them." One woman came in, selected fabric from swatches, gave Witsken a general idea of what she wanted, and commented, "Most of my friends go to New York for their clothes and they all look alike. I don't have time to do that, and the things you've made for me have gotten many compliments." Witsken says "They trust me to make them look beautiful and are willing to spend the money on custom sewn clothing."

A recurring problem in custom sewing is that of the customer who simply has to have their garment made or altered immediately. Witsken deals with this by stating her policy on all printed materials and on the wall of her shop: she charges a 50% surcharge for rush orders. It makes the client think twice about whether the job is really that important, and compensates Deanna for the extra hours she might have to schedule.

Concierge Services

Leah Crain originally had a storefront business, then moved to a workroom over the retail bridal shop that provided most of her business. However, after more than four years of successful operation she moved out of state to be married. Instead of going to the expenses of opening yet another store, Leah contracted with several office buildings to provide alteration's services to their tenants.

Every week, Crain makes the rounds to these buildings, picking up articles to be altered, and delivering completed work. The concierge service provided by building management handles payment of her fees. They also provide Leah with a space for measuring, fitting, and pinning hems. In return, the concierge agency takes a percentage as a commission. The details are all spelled out in contracts with the concierge. Originally tendered to her in "boilerplate" form, some of the contract terms were not agreeable to Crain, so she had them modified before the final signing. Of particular concern was a clause that entitled the concierge service to a commission from *any* revenue generated by her in *any* of their buildings, whether there was a service operating there or not. It so happened that one of their downtown buildings was being considered as a location by a store that is one of her biggest clients. If Leah had not noticed this troublesome provision in the contract, fees generated from that site would have been subject to her agreement with the concierge. The store never located there. But it could have cost Leah significantly each year. This story has a moral: read contracts carefully, or have your attorney look them over.

Crain's association with this store was the result of a referral from their previous alterations' specialist, who was retiring. She says she gets a lot of her business this way. She enjoys her work with the stores, because it is so hassle free. Clerks do the pinning and billing – she just picks up the work and delivers it by the agreed upon time.

Good Advice

The advice of **Mary Tomlinson** to anyone interested in an alterations business is: "Many women who are interested in doing this type of work seem to be under the impression that because they can sew and like it, they can sew for the public. This couldn't be more out of touch! It takes a great deal of skill and experience to take on the public – too many take on projects they can't handle, won't admit it, and ruin the customer's clothes. We see these horrors everyday, coming from all areas of the country."

Tomlinson, together with her daughter **Deborah Coston**, have operated an alterations' business in Clemson, South Carolina, for the past sixteen years, including four in a shopping center storefront. When Mary first arrived in the area, there were still seamstresses who traveled from home to home, sewing for families in exchange for room and board. "They had no other home, so they were at the mercy of those for whom they worked," Tomlinson says. "They really didn't make any money, either." Bucking this tradition, Debbie and Mary have slowly but consistently raised their rates to a level that allows them to make a decent living.

Of the way they perform their work, Mary says this: "We always put the alterations back in the manner the manufacturer created it – hems, seams, etc. We don't reinvent the wheel, and we don't rip everything; we do half at a time, so we have the original as a pattern. We never 'correct' the original. Seamstresses can learn a lot from observing the many different methods of designing and creating clothes. There are many good techniques from manufacturers not taught in Home Economics.

"It takes a great deal of intelligence to do this work. Many people tend to discount this and don't appreciate the skill it takes to make clothes fit the wide variety of bodies people walk around in. Not everyone can or should take on this responsibility; the general public is not unreasonable, but many have experienced poor work. My advice is to learn and be open to new methods and be conservative in all changes. We rarely 'cut off' – you can't correct what is gone."

Chapter 3

Custom Design: Square Dance/Western wear, Special Needs

Square Dance & Western Wear

Trends in design create business opportunities for those in the right place at the right time, and for those already dabbling in this field when it becomes trendy. The current popularity in Western and square dancing, and the skyrocketing number of line dancing clubs has created high demand for proper Western attire.

Doogie Stewart is riding high in the saddle with Western wear. With a background in costume design and a degree from the theater department of the University of Cincinnati, Doogie began working with local theater groups on their costume needs. Of course he sewed for himself all the time, too. At a jamboree for country line dancers, so many people complimented him on his self-designed shirts that he got the idea for a custom-made Western wear business.

A trip to the local SCORE office netted Stewart "no advice worth having", from the first representative he spoke with, so he requested another counselor. The advisor assigned to him, a former bra manufacturer, advised Doogie to invest in industrial machines to speed up his production, mass-produce his shirts, and buy all his supplies wholesale. Buying bulk goods at a reduced cost has helped him realize a greater profit margin, but he is not convinced about mass production, at least not for his business.

Armed with a book of sample bodies and fabrications, Stewart takes orders for custom-made, and often one-of-a-kind shirts. It is important to him to personalize his designs to suit his customer's needs, and he believes he is offering a unique service. His fabrics are pre-washed to reduce shrinkage, and he offers the options of double-stitched seams, strengthened for "riding, roping or fiddling". Right now he is targeting the "square" of four couples in a square dance group who wish to have coordinated shirts. To this end, Doogie is getting more active in the local square dance circles.

To Doogie, "cowboy clothes" mainly means shirts, but fancy, frilly skirts and ruffled tops of women's square dance outfits also offer a great possibility for sewing profit. Unusual dance clothing is difficult to find, and competitive dancers like to look different from the other contestants. At the 41st Annual Square Dance Convention held in Cincinnati, Ohio in June 1992, there were more than 25,000 participants. The sheer variety in the color and fabric combinations of all those swirling skirts made heads swim. Patterns and tracing paper were available in the "sewing room". Other than the dance area where the contestants were, this was the busiest room in the Convention Center. However, many of the dancers don't sew; they were tracing patterns for someone else to have their own designs made. Opportunities abound for the savvy custom sewing pro who has access to, or interest in this market.

Special Needs

Another overlooked opportunity lies in the special needs' market. Although hospital garb is one of the first markets that springs to mind, the trend towards home nursing and independence in health care has generated many new markets for sewn goods. Niche marketing may find you mass producing products for this area, or creating custom garments for temporary special needs, such as maternity clothing appropriate for the office. After the baby is born, nursing mothers also need practical clothing.

Custom Maternity Clothing

When one of her customers got pregnant, and couldn't find appropriate business clothing that fit, **Janith Bergeron** designed some for her. "Things with little bows on them can't be worn in the boardroom," she says. Many of her customers were executives then in their late 20's to mid-30's beginning a mini boom of career-delayed first pregnancies. Since Janith was already making their work clothes, they naturally turned to her when their special need for maternity clothing could not be met elsewhere.

Bergeron used top-of-the-line silks and woolens her clients could wear through three seasons. She modified commercial patterns to design very wearable garb. Actually, they wore too well, which meant that replacements weren't necessary for her customer's second pregnancies. This was great for her clients but not so good for Janith's business. However, as her father told her "People need to feel good about what they are spending on your product," and Janith agrees.

"It has been a challenge designing for a possibility: pregnant women, even those who have had babies before, do not have a clue as to what their shape will be at their maximum size. Some of these ladies have surprised me with how big they've gotten," Janith says. Well-proportioned slim women take longer to sew for; she can't figure out where to put the ease quite as readily. "I've been fighting my own curvaceousness for years; I *know* where to put the ease for my figure!"

Bergeron's ultimate goal is to create her own line of professional-looking maternity wear. Toward this end, she is learning more about pattern design, patternmaking, and drafting. Speed is important, too, to keep the profit margin fat enough to make custom designing worthwhile. To further increase her margin, Bergeron tries to use wholesale fabric whenever she can. Frequently, a fabric store in her hometown of Dover, New Hampshire, orders bolts of fabric for her. Eventually, she hopes to order her own directly from the manufacturer, and have a storefront with specialty fabrics.

Janith attended an American Buyer's Market show in Boston with a friend. Seeing the sale booths of several small clothing manufacturers, Bergeron decided to present her own line at such a show, and she's actively working towards that goal. It's been difficult to find stitchers in her area, and she hopes to start a referral network or a dressmaker's cooperative for sewing professionals. This would help boost not only her own business, but the economy of the area. Many people in the New England states were forced into working from home in recent years because a number of seacoast businesses have either left the area, or have simply gone out of existence. Janith laments, "Companies were bareboneing it, and not giving themselves enough profit margin to take care of business. One out of three of the people I know are out of work. In New Hampshire, the world is up for sale, and at a very low price. It's very difficult to get a loan, and even harder to find customers who have money to spend." Janith is still getting a great deal of satisfaction by meeting the clothing requirements for those who come to her with their particular needs.

Nursing Home Clothing

"Our business started out of the heart of our love for our parents," says **Pat McRight**, of Austin, Texas. She and her lifelong friend **Doris Gathright** are partners in Tu-Rights Creations, a manufacturer and pattern design company of garments for special needs. When Gathright's 88-year old mother was admitted to a nursing home, clothing became a big problem. Her inability to dress herself and the immodesty she endured when she was dressed in the garb traditional for nursing home patients, was devastating to her dignity. Doris looked around for more intelligently designed and attractive garments. The clothing displayed in ready-to-wear catalogues seemed ugly and skimpy. Despite extensive search, she could never find anything that her mother could put on and take off easily or painlessly. After her mother passed away, Doris and her friend Pat McRight began in earnest to design and perfect patterns for improved garments for the elderly. Naming their company after the "right" in each of their names (they each married into the names!), they set out to work on what they felt to be an urgent need for nursing home patients.

Accustomed to sewing for themselves, they had few patternmaking skills. Nevertheless, they felt compelled to go ahead with designing a "dignity dress". With a full overlap in the back, this unique garment provided a full, non-binding feeling, with a much greater degree of privacy than the typical hospital gown. Easy-closing Velcro tabs made the wearer feel secure, yet allowed easy on and off for stiff fingers. "When people put a loved one in a nursing home, they often can't afford the additional financial burden of buying expensive clothing. Patterns offer a way to make attractive, useful garments at a lower cost," says Pat McRight. "There's a lot of discrimination against people with disabilities. As time goes on, and we have more older people in the general population, the need for this type of clothing will be recognized." Pat also suggests that mastectomy patients might need special clothing, an issue they may address in the future.

The two "Rights" are "going at a pace we feel we can handle", and are looking for ways to expand the marketing range of their patterns beyond the Southern states where they are now mainly available. Making some sample garments, they discovered how versatile they were. Meanwhile, Tu-Rights has been selling the ready-made garments to pharmacies. "People are delighted to find them," says McRight. Mass production is not yet in the picture because of the difficulty in finding consistent and dependable contractors. They tried, but one manufacturer put the Velcro strips in the wrong place, and they had to "sit and rip them all forever" .

"We have to keep this in front of people, so that when they need it, they can find it" says Pat McRight. Their patterns are sold in fabric stores, including the Wynn's and Crafts, Etc. chains. A firm in Austin, Texas prints their patterns; they also provide a folding service. To represent the love that spurred Doris and Pat to design the patterns, they use intertwined hearts as their logo, and all the matching points on the patterns, normally shown by triangles, are charmingly represented by hearts.

With the aid of their supportive spouses, they drew out their designs for the logo and advertising materials. Pat's husband "worked out the fuzzies from my stick figures," she says. With the aid of a container shop in Austin, they designed an in-store display box for the patterns. After dismissing the idea of shrink-wrapping as too unfriendly, they chose to use ziptop plastic bags for packaging.

Tu-Rights got a huge break when "Modern Maturity" magazine ran a feature article about the duo. Mail response to that feature, forwarded to Tu-Rights in Texas, was gratifying, and generated a number of orders. A subsequent mention in *Threads* magazine also produced interest. Along the way, Pat says, they have "learned a lot: how to market, how to make contacts." She says that neither she nor Doris have any problem asking questions, which has served them well, and helped them promote their "labor of love" to ease the last years of life in some small way.

Chapter 4

Bridal & Formalwear

Custom Bridal

The glamorous world of bridal lace with its elegant satins and silks is quite appealing to those considering a career in sewing. But as a specialty, sewing for weddings can be fraught with headaches for the unsuspecting.

Neighbors and friends often ask the only sewing expert they know to make a wedding gown or some bridesmaids' dresses for them, thus launching the start of many a dressmaker into businesses. Too often, her inexperience causes her to undercharge. Or, because the customer is a friend or relative, she just wants to do them a favor. Unfortunately, this attitude carries over to her other business dealings.

Weddings are a time of peak emotions for the bride, and often for the bride's mother as well. In fact, the bridal specialist may find herself dealing more with the mother than with an overwhelmed daughter. Often, the mother is playing out a long-held fantasy of what she always dreamed of for her daughter's wedding; occasionally, the mother is acting out a fantasy of what she wishes her own wedding had been. To deal with this, **Debbie Coston** simply sends the mothers away. Debbie feels that having mothers there only intimidates brides-to-be, based on the change in personalities she often observes when the moms leave.

On the other hand, sometimes the mother's presence can work to the dressmaker's advantage. "I encourage the mother to be there. In the case of an indecisive bride, *somebody* needs to make a decision," says Karen Howland. This is especially true if there's a difference of opinion – sometimes a bride takes the opposite tack just to annoy her mother, regardless of what she really wants.

Due to the stress connected with this otherwise happy time, **Kathi Crean** of Maryland holds firm to her policy of completing the wedding gown 6 to 8 weeks prior to the wedding date. This allows time for unanticipated emergencies, and gives Kathi leeway when scheduling. Currently, she books nearly a year ahead. (Among most of the dressmakers interviewed for this book, an average lead time for the complete project is 6 months.)

Though Crean finds bridal design work rewarding, she notes that economic pressures are changing the character of her business. Lately, brides have been buying their gowns off the rack at the retail and outlet stores, then coming to her for alterations. This saves them money, and actually is a more profitable use of Kathi's time, as it is less labor intensive for her. She feels that, due to the long lead time of weddings (some are planned as much as two years in advance), it takes longer for fluctuations in the economy to affect her business. Bridal shops, with their intense sales pressure, don't care of their customers after the sale. That's where Kathi comes in.

Originally, Crean worked in her parent's basement, which was not set up to receive clients. Fortunately at the time she was managing a needlework shop, which allowed her to take in dressmaking jobs, and gave her a shop environment for her dressmaking. Kathi slowly built up her business, working 6-8 hours a week, in addition to her full-time job. Even better, down the street was a high school, and Crean drew many prom and homecoming dress assignments from there. Eventually, as these young customers grew up, they came to her for their wedding gown needs.

When Crean received a proposal it came with the news that her fiance was being transferred out of state. This presented a dilemma for Kathi, who had invested seven hard years in her business. Love prevailed, and she was glad to make the choice to move, resigning herself that it would take another seven years of building a new business. However, it only took her one year to build it back to where it had been. Learning from her previous mistakes, she got established right away, specializing in bridal. Now that Kathi is expecting a baby, she anticipates working at a different pace, making use of nights and weekends when her husband is able to take a turn at child care. This will be a total change for her, as she has been accustomed to working weekday hours (7:00 A.M. to 7:00 P.M.) the whole time she's been in business. She also hopes to have someone come to her home to care for the baby, and continue to maintain a professional atmosphere.

It's been said that bridal is a "branching" business; once a dressmaker sews a bridesmaid's dress, the young woman will want the same designer to make her wedding gown. She'll also make recommendations to friends who are getting married. This is especially effective with those who are "always a bridesmaid, never a bride"!

The perennial bridesmaid launched **Karen Howland** into business. She had been making bridesmaid's gowns for another dressmaker, who only made custom bridal gowns, and referred all the attendants to Howland. When the bridesmaids began to get married, they called Karen for their gowns, since she had already done work for them. The other bridal designer was so busy that there was plenty of work for two designers in the same area.

Previous experience at a bridal shop had given Howland access to fitting hundreds of different body shapes. It was an excellent foundation when she decided to start her own bridal design and custom sewing business from her home in Loveland, Ohio. Five children, and the need to be there for them, was the determining factor in her decision to come home to work. Although she once thought this would be a temporary arrangement until all her children were in school, Karen now makes a career out of sewing. Remodeling her garage gave her a workroom separate from the rest of the house.

Making her own patterns gives Howland the freedom to exercise her incredibly creative mind. She admits that sometimes her imagination goes beyond economic feasibility. She has made a couture quality gown just to see the finished product, while only charging her client for a plainer, more pedestrian creation. This may not make good financial sense in the short term, but it has helped give Karen a reputation as a very special bridal designer. Her fame in this area has led to more contracts than if she had stuck to more run-of-the-mill styles. Karen says for many brides, this is their first time working with a dressmaker. They often want a unique garment, and not necessarily in their normal style. "There's a high need for this type of dressmaker," says Howland.

Crinoline rental has offered Karen a way to increase her profit margin. She schedules rental dates on her calendar so she knows when the slips will be in use. Her major problem with this sideline is storage – crinolines take up a lot of space, and Howland has little to spare. Also near her consultation area, a beautiful display of gloves, headpieces and fur wraps graces one wall of her shop, attracting a good deal of attention. Karen designed the faux fur wraps for those brides who plan to wear off-the-shoulder gowns, but their weddings may take place in chilly or inclement weather. Some of the styles fit nicely over the exaggerated sleeves of many gowns.

Marketing

In order to attract new business, **Liz Burkhart** of LB Creations sends letters to newly engaged young women, getting her leads from the engagement notices in her local paper. Community newspapers often have this information. (Another source of names could be an area jeweler.) Her letter, "Congratulations on your engagement", informs the prospective bride that she needs to choose a dress as soon as possible, since the whole tone of the wedding depends on her choice of dress. The letter also hints that the bride should have custom-designed attendants' clothing. At the end of the flyer, Liz asks for the sale by urging the potential customer to make an early appointment. A few months later, Liz sends a follow-up letter to the bride-to-be, who by now has probably been to some retail bridal shops, and might be dissatisfied with the dresses she's seen there. Once again, Burkhart asks her prospective client to call for a consultation. This letter campaign has been successful in generating business for Liz.

When clothing is picked up, a thank you tag is attached, with an invitation to call again for more work. Of course, LB Creations' number is prominently displayed on the tag! Liz also had "thank you for the referral" cards printed, which is a sound business idea. You can never thank people too many times.

Another way to get bridal business contacts is by participating in regional bridal shows. An opportunity to meet hundreds of prospective customers and sharing a booth with related professionals could work to your advantage. One bridal designer who had a booth at a Washington, DC area show garnered enough new business for a year. (see Chapter 14 for more information on exhibiting at shows.)

Storefront Bridal Business

Like many sewing pros, **Joyce Hittesdorf** began working from her home because she had small children. Also, her husband was trying to finish school and hold down a job. By the time they had three children, Joyce was sewing at home 25-30 hours a week. In time, her husband's salary became sufficient to support the family, so Joyce closed her business to devote more time to the kids. That is, until the inflation of 1976, and an unfortunate string of hardships forced Joyce to again augment the family income.

Since Joyce had been at home with the kids for so many years, she was understandably uncertain about her job skills. She put a sewing ad in the paper, though, and left her name with two local fabric stores. Almost overnight, she was very successfully back in the sewing business.

After a while, Hittesdorf began turning down alterations (which she didn't like), concentrating only on dressmaking. She hired a high school girl to cut patterns for her, and to do simple handwork. Everything was going well, when her husband Mike became the president of his company. With this promotion came a big raise, and a move to Indianapolis. With her roots pulled up, Joyce didn't sew for others for some time. Then, while volunteering during a Marriage Encounter weekend, a fellow volunteer mentioned that she was opening a bridal shop. During the ensuing discussion she asked Joyce to do her alterations for her.

Within a year, the owner had Hittesdorf making custom gowns for the shop. Joyce felt the owner was taking advantage of her talents, and quit. Through word of mouth, Joyce began building her own business, making gowns for former customers and their friends. By 1986 her business had grown to the point where she was keeping two employees busy. By 1988 **Mike Hittesdorf** was spending 20 hours a week helping her with her paperwork. The constant comings and goings of her patrons became too obvious in their quiet suburban Indianapolis neighborhood. In 1989 they opened a 1,250 square foot shop in an office park. A consultation room, a fitting room, and workrooms were carved out of the apartment-like setting. The continuation of the home atmosphere, so appealing to her customers, was a good move according to Hittesdorf. In nine months, they had grown large enough again to necessitate another move to a 2,500 square foot condo in the same complex.

Branching Out

By now, Hittesdorf had hired more help, and was selling bridal accessories from her larger space. She was also still "running to fabric stores to buy 30 yards of fabric for gowns." One day while fabric shopping, she looked on the end of several fabric bolts, wrote the manufacturers' information on her hand, and went home and called a couple of companies for ordering information. "At first they just laughed at me," she explains. With persistence, she finally got someone to listen to her. She began carrying bolts of satins and other bridal fabrics to sell to her customers, eliminating the middleman, and increasing her profit margin.

Joyce also custom dyes white laces that need to be off-white or ivory. She began doing this after calling a manufacturer for some off-white lace, and learning they had to dye it before sending it to her. Her formula for ivory is instant tea and Rit Yellow. (The tea alone is too pink.) Mike, who had by now joined Joyce full time, began taking a more active role in the business, ordering stock, and taking care of taxes. When their local fabric store went out of business, they expanded their own fabric department further

Brides wanting crinolines for the more voluminous gowns were getting the run-around by bridal shops who had not sold them the gowns, so Joyce found a source for them wholesale. A minimum order of three got her started. Fabric shoes were another logical addition to her accessory stock.

By October of 1989, five full-time and two part-time employees, including Joyce and Mike, were sharing the shop space. One of her employees moved to the area from out of town, just to work with Joyce. "I was honored by that," says Hittesdorf. Her fame has grown locally, too, though they have done very little advertising. In the first year, they didn't even have a Yellow Pages ad, but now they have a "real business". In 1992 they had two phone lines; in 1994 they added a third to handle Visa and MasterCard needs.

Attitude is Everything

"A lot of what's happened in my business is because I've striven to be very professional in what I do," says Hittesdorf. Joyce and her staff present themselves in an efficient and competent manner. "Most brides are in the 25-35 age range, and are out in the business world; they expect a professional attitude. Her wedding day is the most important day in a woman's life." Joyce also tries to get the word out that they do other work in addition to special occasion and bridal. After all, the name of the business is "Something Wonderful!". They strive to branch out to pageant, Mother of the bride, Mother of the groom, and ballroom dance needs, and want more customers looking for "unique clothing".

"I want my employees to do things my way," says Joyce. "We start them out with 'baby steps'. I've perfected ways that produce good quality, but are quick, too." Responsibilities are added in small increments. The "seamstress pool" at Something Wonderful currently boasts two women who can do tailoring. Joyce is still checking their work, because her name is on the front door. Her goal is to bring these employees along to the point where they can do all the tailoring on their own.

Mike and Joyce have a management meeting with their employees once a week, and solicit their help in cutting costs. Through the use of time sheets, they keep close tabs on the costs of each job. Since their objective is to provide "bridge" quality clothing to their customers while continuing to pay a good wage to the employees, keeping the expenses down helps the Hittesdorfs pass these savings on. This dramatically improves employee relations.

To remain current with trends in fashion and color, Joyce's reading list includes W, Women's Wear Daily, Management, Mirabella, Sew News and Threads. She saves forecast trends, and when she goes to market, she looks for the future trends, rather than the current ones, with an eye to being more fashion conscious than the average fabric store. Fashion magazines are in the waiting room of the shop so the customer knows that "it's not a pattern magazine place." Joyce says many of her customers come to her saying "I don't know anything about sewing." She tells them "That's okay; I do."

(In 1994, Joyce and Mike Hittesdorf expanded their business even more: to include a full-fledged fabric store. For more information on this process, see Chapter 23.)

Pageant Gowns

Beauty pageant contestants "spend more money than brides," says **Kathi Crean**, who like Joyce Hittesdorf, also makes pageant gowns. Aside from beauty contests, which is the first type of pageant that comes to mind, other competitions, like majorette and baton twirling, often have a modeling competition included in the judged activities. "They want their garments to glitter on stage; they keep adding on and adding on, which costs more," says Crean. With pride, Kathi points out her clients consistently win honors. Many of the winners have gone on to other, bigger contests – often taking their favorite dressmaker's creations with them.

The annual "500 Ball", one of the two big social events in Indianapolis, gives Joyce Hittesdorf quite a bit of pageant business year. After the Miss Ball State pageant there is usually a flurry of interest in gowns for the evening gown competition. According to Hittesdorf, they don't generally start with her shop. "The girls are chosen five weeks before the event. They spend two weeks shopping for a dress, and one week is lost to spring break, which leaves two weeks to work on a dress." Most of the pageant winners are college students, and sometimes their talent specialty requires yet another gown. "They have extremely short deadlines, and fitting must be to perfection, so there's a lot of stress with this kind of work."

After five years of working with pageant contestants, Joyce knows what looks good on stage, and what colors are most effective. The perspective of the runway from below, where the judges generally sit, makes a difference in the designs Hittesdorf might recommend. Also, the various pageants have quite specific rules and written criteria for dress. The girls often rely on Joyce for advice on sitting and walking in their gowns. Also, because the kind of jewelry that is most dramatic on stage was largely unavailable, Something Wonderful began stocking some for their pageant customers. With her knowledge of what looks best on stage, she is especially proud of a spectacular dress she designed for the debut of an opera singer of larger than average proportions. The singer flew back and forth between New York and Indianapolis for her fittings.

Another niche is sewing for the Junior Miss Pageants. Hittesdorf calls the clothes "fussy dresses", of the kind that you wouldn't ordinarily put on a child. She begins most often by asking the mother of the contestant, "What did the winner wear last year?" Then she tells them to bring in pictures of the type of creation they envision.

Dance wear

What kind of formal dress requires exposing the feet of the wearer? According to Joyce Hittesdorf, it's a ballroom dancing contest gown. The movements of the feet are important criteria the judges use when grading the dancers. The sleeves of the garments need to move freely so the shoulder movements are also visible to the judges. As the level of competition reached by the dancer increases, there are more stringent demands for their costumes. At the higher levels, the dress must fit the dance. Joyce designed one dress for a lower level dancer that she could continue to use as she advanced in competition. Knowing these requirements allowed Hittesdorf to advise her client, and helped her save money. "I love ostrich feathers," says Joyce, and she likes to incorporate them in her designs.

Eveningwear

Living in a resort town affords **Juliene Goins** a variety of eveningwear design opportunities. Because of the higher income range of her customer base, Goins makes many types of evening clothing, including capes and dressy coats. Creating this type of clothing carries with it some special problems. The one-time wearing nature of the garments makes them a little risky: the occasion might be canceled, the wearer-to-be could get sick, or the very expense of the clothing may create buyer's remorse. The potential client then panics, and asks for the fabric back. Accordingly, Juliene asks for a 50% deposit, and if she provides any of the supplies, she charges the client for those as well. The customer does not take the garment from the shop until the remainder of the bill is paid. She also saves the scraps, then uses them to create accessory items for sale in her shop. (Not everyone recommends this practice; some advise giving the customer back all the leftover fabric, unless they specifically say they don't want it.)

Accessories

Designing and creating bridal accessories like headpieces, garters, ringbearer pillows, and handbags can generate substantial profits. **Claudia Lynch**, of Sideline Design in Cleveland, has added just such a specialty to her business. When arts funding declined in 1991, the costume business she had built up for many years was no longer paying the bills (see Chapter 8). At first, Claudia thought she would move into the bridal business, but then she realized that she would have to deal with brides, which was not her cup of tea. Fiddling around with the scraps from some bridal-type fabric and some of the tulle Lynch had stockpiled from her tutu production, she decided to try a few styles of headpieces. Having worked as a milliner's assistant many years before, she had training that "I didn't appreciate at the time." Taking her designs around to some local shops, she got such strong response that she developed a total of fifteen styles to sell. This eventually increased to the thirty fashions in her current line. Lynch now takes the line to bridal markets, wholesaling to retailers.

Cotillions and debutante balls offer other chances to sew the glamorous gowns that are mandatory for such state occasions. In some areas, the cultural traditions of various ethnic groups require special clothing for various functions. Some First Communion or graduation gowns are quite elaborate, as are the coming-of-age party dresses for daughters of traditional Hispanic/Latino families, who celebrate this event.

Chapter 5

Lingerie to Outerwear

Lovely to Look at

With catalogues landing in our mailboxes filled with pretty undies, and a Victoria's Secret store in every mall, fancy lingerie has become big business and it seems there's room to grow.

When **David and Kristina Bonfield** met on a squash court in China, he was a British geophysicist working for an oil company there, and she was a diplomat for the US to China. After they got married in 1987, they took a week-long, winter train trip on the Siberian Express, from China to Siberia, by way of Mongolia. The train was unheated, but they soon found their knit silk, Chinese long underwear kept them cozily warm.

The Bonfields settled in London in 1988, where Kristina took up her diplomat duties once again. David had had enough of being a scientist, and decided to import those Chinese longjohns to sell in his country. They bought 1,000 each of the bottoms and tops in various sizes, and advertised in various magazines and newspapers. Soon they expanded the line to include men's silk jersey briefs and vests (sleeveless undershirts, or singlets).

David Bonfield took a rudimentary pattern drafting class, read a few books, and set out to make patterns and samples for some basic items. These were sent to China, where they were then turned into four styles. At the same time, silk was becoming cheaper and more common in stores in England, and was growing more difficult for the Bonfields to find from their former suppliers.

In order to make their initial samples themselves, they bought an overlocker and a domestic sewing machine. Setting up in the dining room, David taught himself to sew, and ran up Kristina's designs. By now, their Body Aware company had a color catalogue with 40-50 items. The Chinese factories were becoming unreliable, however. "No matter what we sent them, the garments came back different than we designed them. It made no difference to send samples," says David. They looked in England for CMT's – Cut, make and trim shops, which are small factories – to make their goods. This worked for a while, but the cost of subcontracting was too high.

In 1991, the Bonfields bought some used industrial machines and hired two operators. The overlocker, elasticator, binder and cover stitch machines were set up in the Bonfield dining room. Kristina designed all the garments, while David did the pattern grading and cutting. "We didn't have dinner guests for a few months," says David. "When Kristina had our first baby, we had to find a more spacious workspace. Since then, we've never looked back." They eventually moved twice more before they landed in their current factory.

Their business is 90% mail order; retail shops sell the rest of their goods. Body Aware is just one of their labels, specializing in men's underwear. The English Naturals line has very soft, lovely women's lingerie in the European tradition. There are three other men's lines, including Aprés Noir which features more exotic designs like velvet/Lycra briefs. American Built features Kristina's activewear designs. The name reflects the attractiveness of American products to the British.

Currently, Body Aware's 5,000 square foot factory in England has 50-60 machines, 2 cutters, and 30-40 stitchers, called "machinists" in the UK They also have a separate mail order fulfillment operation. However, the Bonfields themselves have moved out of England to Kristina's native California. They import garments into the US from their factory at present, with plans to build a factory here in the US. "We're not keen on using cheap labor any more, after our experience with the undependable labor force in China," says David. They hope to repeat their British success story here – in 1994, Kristina won a television competition to find Britain's best and most promising business. As David says: "We were up against all sorts of glamorous hi-tech businesses, but there we were with our low tech sewing machines beating the lot of them!"

Custom Lingerie

Although today's lingerie is lovely and available at many stores, people who fall outside the "normal" range as defined by the retail industry may have a hard time finding their size. Often ignored by manufacturers, wearers of larger sizes would still like feminine and silky lingerie and sleepwear. Typical sizing in many stores runs from Small to Extra Large. It is not unusual for the queen-sized woman to need sizes 2X to 4X, so a market exists for pretty, sexy day- and nightwear. And as David Bonfield points out, men don't always fit into department store sizes, either. Conversely, those who wear very small sizes also have a tough time finding what they need. If you can or like to sew this sort of garment, this area might present a profitable business for you.

Sewing custom bras for those with hard to fit bodies, or unusual needs became **Beverly Ledwith's** mainstay. She has some background in special needs sewing, when a friend with unusual measurements could no longer find her favorite undergarments. The friend had a bustline of 44" couple with ribcage, waist and hip circumferences of 27", yielding a commercial bra size of a 28L. Since the client was a professional who gave talks all over the country, she was desperate to find something that fit her.

Ledwith could not find the extra wide straps and back hook sets necessary to support the framework of such a garment. Finally she went to the local Goodwill store hoping to find parts of used bras that she could launder and use in a new garment (with her customer's permission). Ledwith made the happy discovery of several (new) discontinued models of the very bra the client needed! Of the 14 bras she bought (for $25), some of the sizes fit, some didn't, so she plundered the unusable styles for parts. The customer's daughter, having the same figure problem, also became a customer. This launched Bev into business.

There are some inherent challenges with this specialty. According to Ledwith, garments cannot be tried on until they are completed, and they are very labor intensive. Also, people who have never gotten a good fit often do not recognize it when they do get it, and consequently can be difficult to deal with.

Activewear

Related to lingerie, and directly connected to the advance in stretch fabrics, the exercise wear market has exploded. Swimwear, once only available in sizes dictated by those few companies who made it for retail stores, has come into its own as a custom sewing specialty.

The Ultimate Fit, a Paso Robles, California store, specializes in custom, computer-fitted swimwear. Owner **Carol McNellis** uses a special computer fitting process licensed from Second Skin Swimwear of Florida. Using a video capture of the customer wearing one of the 30 basic styles, Carol traces body contours. The computer program "measures" the body, based on both the digitized figure and the various measuring points McNellis designates (high hip, full bust, etc.). A pattern is created and printed by the computer, then cut and sewn by McNellis in her store in the style and fabric the customer has chosen.

Patterns are made on Pellon yardage, then filed by customer number. When the customer is ready for another suit, McNellis simply applies the pattern to the new garment. Some basic patterns and sizes are on file (in unusual sizes) for use in solving challenging fit situations. "Most of the time, suits fit right off the bat," says McNellis. "At $100 a suit, I can't make money when the customer comes back three or four times." Sometimes, the issue is not really the fit; the customer may have buyer's remorse when she gets home with such an expensive purchase.

Because of the nature of the business, McNellis's shop has limited hours. Since she has to do most of the sewing herself, she offers appointments for fitting, with hours and phone numbers printed on her shop door. Her business tends to be busier in the summer, just as it would be anywhere else.

Skating Costumes

An accomplished custom designer of costumes of all types, **Ursula Jones** specializes in skating outfits and swimwear. Growing up in Missoula, Montana, as the daughter of the deputy sheriff (and living in quarters next door to the jail!), Ursula learned to sew as an economic measure. Exposure to beading, taught to her by a Native American neighbor, was to come in handy in later life. A double college major in voice and piano led to a job after graduation as an assistant professor at Eastern New Mexico State University. She had listed "sewing" on her resume as a hobby, and because of this, "the dean told me to take care of the school's theater costumes. It was a big job, as no one had organized them in years."

Soon, Ursula found herself sewing costume for the school's stage productions. One year, she and two others made over 500 costumes. "I was the first to use French-cut legs in a production," she says. She learned to sew better, and faster, but without the fine finishing techniques she had been taught. "It was hard to come back to quality sewing after that".

When she married Nick Jones, a young Air Force officer, they began moving around the country. In San Antonio, Ursula began making costumes for her daughter Nicole, who was busy with gymnastics, dance classes, and swimming. The long-waisted figure of her daughter forced her to learn to make bathing suits. Along the way, Jones became an expert in designing with stretch fabrics.

A few years after they moved to Cincinnati, Jones found herself in a local fabric store being asked "You look like you know what you're doing; can you help me with this skating costume?" This launched Ursula into her current costume business. (Her original customer is still coming to her with orders for her daughter, who is a champion skater.) Skills she has acquired throughout her life – beading, stretch fabric sewing, and designing for physically active performers – have all combined to give Jones a special edge in her field. She also has a good sense of what looks the most dramatic from afar for skaters. Beads, sequins and other glitzy details, combined with the use of floaty details that move with the skater, all add up to pizzazz. These same skills are applicable to dance costumes for ballet, tap and jazz dancers.

Outerwear

On the opposite end of the clothing spectrum, outerwear offers a chance for profits, too. Skiwear, in its infinite variations, is a potential moneymaking area. Other outerwear options include hiking and camping gear, and clothing for fishing, hunting and other outdoor activities. With the popularity of jogging and the fitness craze in general, smaller, more flexible companies were able to fulfill the needs of the hobbyists in each field much quicker than their larger, and less nimble colleagues.

When her children were small, **Janet Pray** wanted to make some money by sewing, so she began making things to sell at street fairs. One of her most successful products was a pieced lace vest. Wearable art and sportswear that she branded with her own unique twist also sold well, but she wanted to specialize in something.

In 1980, Janet participated in a Renaissance Festival. She decided to rent a booth when she learned that people paid $8 a head, "just to shop" (now it's $13). Nearly 20,000 people a day attend these shows. She exhibited on a cool fall weekend, and the capes she had recently begun making sold well. They also happened to have the highest gross profit margin of all her products. With a good supplier of wool melton, and a smooth production process, she soon had a wonderful specialty. Janet says she decided to "Keep it simple, stupid" and eliminate the mishmash of products she'd been creating, refining her product line in the process.

Pray was one of the first to use wool melton this way, mostly single layer, and in very simple designs. "Fifteen years ago, no one worked with wool melton. People wanted less expensive, more disposable coats, and good wool melton can last 30 years," she says. The horseshoe-shaped pattern works well, too. They give demonstrations at her booth, showing the versatilities of the design, which can be wrapped, belted, or otherwise dressed up. The timeless design is perfect for the Renaissance venue, because, as Pray says "It could have been worn in Jesus' time, but it looks great over a 1995 suit. We sell them to all sorts of people, including men and young college guys." And knights in shining armor. "It looks great over a knight costume. Very sexy."

One of the secrets to Pray's success with her capes has been manufacturing them in various lengths, from Petite to Extra-Long. "When a 4'11" individual comes into our booth and says 'I've always wanted to wear a cape, but they're all too long,' I can show her the Petite size. They usually end up buying one."

Her coats are simple, unlined and versatile. One style incorporates two colors of melton, and sports handmade buttons. Its large dolman sleeves make it a hit with many customers. In the coat styles, Janet also keeps it simple: she limits her stock to small, medium and large.

Subcontractors

Four people now work for her making coats and capes. Pray precuts the garment, then sends the cut fabric, thread and labels to the workers, all of whom work at home. Each worker is given a specific deadline. Janet contributes her success to properly training the subcontractors in the production techniques that will make them most efficient. "I feel this is unique to my business; they can make the $8-10 per hour I promised by the time they're finished with the third cape," she says. "That's a really important part of how I make this work, rather than having seamstresses who earn only $2-3 an hour." Making sure each worker qualifies as a subcontractor under federal guidelines is another important consideration.

Chapter 6

Custom Tailoring, Menswear, Shirtmaking, Uniforms

Tailoring

When you think of tailoring, does the image of an old man in shirtsleeves and a tie, with a measuring tape around his neck spring to mind? Things are changing these days. The tailor down the street may not even make the garment, or "he" could be a she. If you love the process of shaping garments with steam and sewing, a career in tailoring could be in your future.

Marla Kazell put her experience both as a samplemaker for Stretch & Sew and sewing for a custom tailor into her own business. A part-time job sewing samples in a fabric store gave her referrals from which to build a customer base. Marla turned down all requests for bridal work, preferring instead to concentrate on ladies tailoring. The bridal work was not appealing, especially when she thought about making the same bridesmaids' dress five times. "I would rather work on a gorgeous piece of wool any day," she explains.

Although there is no lack of fabric stores in her area, Kazell carries a line of House of Laird fabrics as a service to her customers. The fabrics are very high quality, and the seasonal collections of about 1,000 selections offer her clients good depth of choice. A 20% commission is a nice bonus to Kazell, though she does not market the service with enough vigor to make it a main profit center of her business. House of Laird charges a small fee to become their representative, and has a minimum order of 1/8 of a yard of each fabric choice. Kazell says her biggest expense, after ordering and advertising, is UPS charges.

Marla's customers are mostly businesswomen, for whom she makes suits, dresses, skirts, blouses, jackets, and some casual things. The use of commercial patterns works for Kazell, because most of her clients fit in them with minor adjustments. For those who don't, she likes to use Burda patterns. Having studied the Roberta Carr method of using Burda patterns, she uses them more like a "custom pattern", and there is usually a style in the current selection that corresponds to her customer's choice.. In Kazell's opinion, the way they are graded makes changes to fit the client easy and logical.

Thirty years of custom sewing gave **Mary Ellen Flury** the tailoring experience that she illustrates so well in her classes and videos. She teaches the techniques she learned to others through her classes, and more recently through her excellent videos on tailoring ladies' and men's jackets, and making men's pants and vests. Aware that the notions and supplies she was recommending in the videos were not widely available, Flury added them to the items she sells by mail order and at shows. (For more on video production and sales, see Chapter 25.)

Custom Shirtmaking

A relative neophyte to the tailoring world, **Eldin Johnston** did custom sewing part-time for co-workers at his job at a New Orleans bank, as well as for others. A walking advertisement for his own work, Eldin is often approached to duplicate his own garments in different fabrications. "Disgusted" with the Bishop method of sewing, Johnston is mostly self-taught. He says he learned by "de-construction", ripping apart ready-made garments in an effort to discover how the method used to construct them.

At first, Eldin had a problem with the way he set up his business; it was too informal at the beginning. "When they know you, it's all very casual; they don't come to fittings on time, they expect you to bring stuff to work." Now he has definite appointments, and controls the pace of the work better. Johnston does all custom work, plus some copying of existing garments. Using a shirt that fits well, Eldin copies the garment and drafts a pattern from it, which he then uses to create new shirts.

Eldin's flair for style received wide recognition with his 1993 winning entry in the design competition of the Fashion Group

International chapter in New Orleans. His unusual entries were of men's skirts in many variations. The business skirt was made like a pair of men's trousers, calf-length, without legs; the collegiate version was fashioned in a tartan plaid with a yoke and button fly; his "street kid" skirt looked like a flannel shirt tied around the waist. A beach skirt rounded out the presentation. All of the designs included coordinating shirts. "They were all very masculine," says Johnston, adding, "there are historical references to skirts for men." According to the entry rules, he had to submit a videotape of his presentation to the judges; Eldin chose to tape each ensemble in its natural habitat: college, office, beach, and street.

Johnston now specializes in shirts, pants and vests. With a little research, he feels confident that he could do a good job on jackets too, but he has not yet attempted one. He has been working for his bank long enough to become fully vested in his pension plan, and Eldin plans to take a distribution of money from the plan and go to New York's prestigious Fashion Institute of Technology for one year. There he hopes to hone his craft and add additional skills to his current repertoire.

Custom Pants

Another tailor who specializes is **Kathleen Spike**, author of *Sew to Success*, the autobiography of her custom sewing business. Kathleen has narrowed her sewing activities to a focus on pants. Having studied the fit of pants for the past 17 years, Spike decided to concentrate on them as an outgrowth of her research. "Well-fitting pants can make anyone look beautiful," she asserts.

Fascinated with the problems inherent in fitting this complicated area of the human body, Spike says she "bought every pants' book and system, looking for the easiest and simplest system of style and fit." Together, Spike figures she spent $10,000 learning style, line and fashion as it applies to pants.

Comfortable she "can fit anyone" in pants, Kathleen hired a graphic artist to design a brochure describing her new service. Spike feels that her current client base appreciates this special service, "investment dressing", as she describes it. An average price of about $250 per pair is what she charges, with the first pair priced somewhat higher to allow for the fitting and patternmaking process. An investment in an industrial machine sped up her sewing processes, without sacrificing the quality she requires.

Since she began this service, Spike, along with Palmer/Pletsch, has produced a video summarizing the method she prefers. (See Sources.)

Made-To-Measure

If you have tailoring skills, and are proficient in selling, but don't want to sew that much, maybe a "made-to-measure" business is for you. **Christine Hoyt** has discovered that she likes this specialty, and has built up quite a following in her Denver location. "I can accelerate a customer's career progress 3-5 years with a better wardrobe and better fit," she says.

Hoyt focuses on made-to-measure, and "cut, trim & make" suits (also referred to as "cut, make and fit"), neither of which requires much sewing by her. For those clients who prefer a less custom garment, Hoyt takes orders for suits that are made using either the customer's fabric, or one chosen from among the many seasonally upgraded swatches she carries. The suits are assembled by a tailoring house, in modified mass production that produces a high quality suit with more hand tailoring than an off-the-rack one would have. A master tailor dictates the designs, and a master cutter dictates the fit.

It takes about six weeks for an order to arrive at Hoyt's shop, when she occasionally has to adjust the fit, to compensate for differences from "off-the-rack" sizing. Some upgrades are available, such as more detailing, finer linings, and horn buttons. Hoyt's suits generally sell for about $575 to $630, which represents "keystone" (double) over wholesale cost, plus postage and charge card percentages. Hoyt tries to maintain a 50% markup to support herself and the shop's overhead.

Her made-to-measure business is a little different. Hoyt can measure a customer for almost any kind of suit. She sends measurements to a made-to-measure house for production of the finished suit in the fabrication, style and specifications chosen by the client. These suits can range in price from $500 to $1,500, depending on the fabric and the workshop. If the suit is benchmade (handmade by an individual tailor) the price is higher, and varies from $1,200 to $5,000. Making a custom suit is very labor intensive. Because few people can afford this luxury, many fine custom tailors have turned to alterations in order to make a living.

Occasionally, the made-to-measure suit requires some slight alterations, usually if the customer has gained or lost weight, but

Christine says men "generally stay pretty consistent". Performing a little nip and tuck provides Hoyt an opportunity to see the customer again and perhaps sell an accessory. An understanding of men's' fit is an important asset in Hoyt's business. "Besides, I think it's wonderful that I can stare at men's behinds all day," she says. Men usually make decisions faster than women, and readily rely on Christine's judgment. Then again, "they don't have nearly the infinite range of choice" that women have.

Hoyt really considers herself a retailer of the tailoring process. Her business is much more service-oriented than most custom sewing concerns. Her business cards are pierced with metal collar stays for an unforgettably distinctive look. The stays are made in India, and nickel-plated by a friend.

In a male-dominated business, Hoyt has faced quite a bit of discrimination, and strives extra hard to present a professional image. Membership in the prestigious Custom Tailors and Designer's Association is part of that effort. At 115 years old, the CTDA is the oldest tailoring association in the country, commanding annual dues of around $200. Every year, their convention in New York draws members from all over the country, including a small number of women members. According to Christine, "Women doing made-to-measure are somewhere below pond scum," but it has not stopped her from actively participating. She points out that dressmakers would not qualify for membership; a working tailoring business is a must.

"I make you pay high prices, and make you wait forever for your clothes. Why do you still come to me?" Hoyt has asked her customers. The answer is her service is invaluable to them, and the male clients seem to respond well to her advice. One thing that bothers her is that respect for her skill is often minimal; doing alterations is often regarded as a finer ability than most sewing.

Made-to-Measure Factory

On the other side of the coin, one of the few made-to-measure houses left in the country is J.B. Simpson, in Cincinnati. A walk through the factory with **Trent Heimann**, son of the owner, was a fascinating, and saddening glimpse into the future of tailoring in the United States. According to both Hoyt and Heimann, the Old World tailors are dying out or retiring, and few are stepping in to replace them. An entire industry that once enjoyed an incredible growth is limping slowly into the sunset.

To set up a made-to-measure tailoring business, Heimann says it is necessary to know fit, (particularly men's, though they also make women's' clothing), to measure accurately, and to have a talent for sales. A good tailor should not need to do much to the suit when it is finished, providing the measurements are accurate.

Several "lines" or swatch collections of varying degrees of quality are available from J.B. Simpson three or four times during the year. They have recently experienced an upsurge in the popularity of the more luxurious grades of wools, cashmeres and other specialty fibers. These lines are provided to the made-to-measure tailors at no cost. If the tailors don't produce orders within a few months, Heimann says he asks if they want to continue to carry the lines, and if so, asked to defray the costs of making and shipping the swatches.

Heimann also echoes Christine Hoyt's belief that women are able to persuade men that their clothes fit, and flatter them with a much greater rate of success than another man. "If a guy's wife comes with him, I know I can sell to him. She'll tell him he needs this and that, and will get him to make a decision. I often just measure the man, then the wife and I go over the styles and fabrics and order the suits together. When he tries on the finished work, we will have better success convincing him of the fit if his wife tells him that it does."

The workshops of J. B. Simpson house over 25 separate businesses that have been assimilated by the parent company, Globe Tailoring. From 120 to 200 employees work on orders received from all over the world, often from notable customers like Lee Iacocca, Perry Como, and many of the golfers touring the pro circuit (in fact, J.B. Simpson makes the prestigious "green jacket" that only winners of the Pro Am can wear). Another important part of the business is for senior pilots of the larger airlines, especially the elite, polished veterans. Perfectly tailored and fitting uniforms ad to their image and stature. This firm also does a brisk business for leaders and dignitaries in other kinds of uniforms, such as those of police captains and chiefs, and even the entire force of some wealthier communities. Riding habits, and uniforms for the Presidential escort are other niches for the tailoring conglomerate.

One reason that Globe Tailoring has survived while others have gone by the wayside is Globe's eagerness to work with retirees. Many former full time employees, unable to earn large amounts of money without sacrificing retirement benefits and Social Security merely work part-time at their specialty. Globe is happy to shape the schedules of these loyal workers, gaining their expertise in tailoring at the same time. Automation of many tasks that were formerly done by many human hands has also helped the company immeasurably.

An enormous Gerber patternmaking machine takes up an entire room, and is handled by one lone computer operator, a task that used to require several skilled people. The customer's measurements are fed into the terminal, along with pertinent information about style, fabric width, and perhaps, stripe or plaid matches. The computer processes the data and sends information to the pattern drawing machine, which is really a tremendous drafting plotter. Pens on the end of the plotter arms draw an accurate pattern, laying the cutlines on a paper layout with a minimum of waste. Next, the paper goes to the cutter, who quickly and lightly irons the layout onto the yardage, then precisely cuts it out. Two workers have replaced many, and the speed of the process produces a tremendous savings to the house. Of course, when circumstances require, some suits and coats are still cut out by hand by a master cutter if the customer chooses.

Depending on how much the client wishes to spend for a truly hand-tailored, or benchmade, garment, the pieces go through the tailoring process, either hand sewn or fused, or by a combination of both. Each article receives constant inspections along the way, from cutting, to sewing, to the many pressings it receives. Heimann asserts that these quality checks are what makes their finished product so superior. Choices of lining fabrics coordinate with matching pocket linings and ties. This helps give the man who is not quite sure of what matches a more pulled-together look. This is especially popular with the many color-blind men who buy from Globe.

Uniforms

A slightly different slant on uniform production is taken by **Rose Ann Barone**. She offers a modified production of school uniforms, including skirts, pants and shorts. There are many commercial uniform houses, but due to automation, they often can't fulfill out-of-the-ordinary orders. For example, a Catholic high school in Barone's area needed pleated wool skirts for their girls in sizes that could not be made by the company that normally supplied them. Some of the students, particularly the younger ones, are quite thin, wearing a size or two smaller than available from the large companies. Rose Ann, who has a bridal dressmaking in Madeira, Ohio, was asked to make all the uniforms for the school. Her shop easily accommodates the fittings required, since it is located only minutes from the school.

Rose Ann is actively seeking a computer program that will allow her to make several patterns economically. She's been cutting each individual pattern separately, and feels her efficiency would greatly improve with automated patterns.

Chapter 7

Furs and Leathers: Faux and Genuine

Furs

Despite the furor over the use of animal skins in clothing, there are still lots of opportunities for those who love to work with either the real thing, or their synthetic counterparts. Furriers are true specialists, and while the scope of this book cannot cover their work, they continue to have a place in the world of sewing. One fur-related enterprise that is gaining popularity in some locales is reworking old coats. A knowledge of furrier techniques is crucial to venture into this type of business.

Recently, however, **Donna Salyers** of Fabulous Furs has revolutionized the glamour world of fur coats with her luxurious faux furs. Back-to-back radio announcements for a fur sale and an exposé on toymakers using kitten fur in place of mink spurred her to make a synthetic fur coat for herself. The subsequent rejection of her newly sewn faux fur as "too valuable to check" in the coatroom of the restaurant at the World Trade Center in New York convinced Donna that she was onto something big. The politically incorrectness of real furs was just then beginning to be a hot public issue. It became apparent to Salyers that there was a market for her discovery, and Fabulous Furs was born in her Cincinnati, Ohio basement.

Moving from the basement, to the family room, to the garage, to an office she rented in one of her husband's buildings, the business took off. Salyers began placing small ads in several national magazines. Packaging the fur yardage with pattern, thread and hard-to-find notions, she sold them as coat kits. At the same time, Donna was still writing a syndicated column she had authored for many years, and continuing to write and produce both a cable TV show and a series of videos for homesewers.

Attracting the attention of movie star Loretta Swit proved to be the media-magnet that propelled Salyers into the public eye in a big way. Swit, one of the stars of the long-running "M.A.S.H." TV series, and an avid animal rights activist, was impressed with the luxurious look and feel of the Fabulous Furs products. Her strong endorsement of the coats gave Donna credibility, and led to appearances on several TV and radio talk shows. Salyers' experience on her TV show "Sewing, Etc." Her natural grace and warmth gave her the aplomb necessary to make the best of these opportunities. "If nobody knows you're out there, you're in trouble," she says. Print coverage in many magazines and newspapers have helped, too. Contributions to charitable organizations connected to animal rights have also paid dividends; Donna's company usually gets a favorable mention by the organizations for its efforts for animal welfare.

In addition to her own coat pattern, Donna soon designed other fur-friendly patterns through Vogue. Some of the designs have been carried in the pattern book. In 1993, Salyers began sending out a beautiful, full-color, 16-page catalogue, with appealing photographs of each coat and jacket style made in various furs. Other products offered in the catalogue include a "pet pack" of stuffed animal patterns (that up those pesky scraps), and the latest addition to the Fabulous Family: Fabu-Leather. This leather look-alike has the stretch and recovery of a knit, with the drape of wool crepe. Its ease of sewing and good looks have made it very popular.

Selling all this fabric requires a lot of space, so Salyers moved into the old Woolworth building in Covington, Kentucky, right across the river from downtown Cincinnati. With a penthouse apartment "over the store", and a couple of floors of wide open space, Donna can get to work right away each day. She starts with a walk with her husband Jim at 6:30 A.M. that serves as an "idea bouncing" session, so right away her mind gets into business mode. In other words, every morning Salyers hits the ground running.

Trying to sell unusual fabrics has made it necessary for Salyers to "hit the road", as well. She travels extensively, demonstrating the sewing techniques for both fur and Fabu-Leather. Rigorous travel schedules like hers are "not for the weak," says Salyers. "It's incredibly hard work. You get there the night before, set up your booth, stagger to bed, and get in your booth by 8:30 the next morning. Of course, you don't eat, but you get a break by doing two seminars a day." Standing in a booth for 12 hours talking to people takes stamina. Barely 5'2", Donna lifts weights all year so she can handle luggage by herself, and "maneuver the circus train," the fur, books and videos that she sells. However, the give and take of conversations with others passionate about sewing energizes her, and she "loves it." Although it takes a "masochistic personality," she keeps signing on for more; the shows are held only a couple of months during the year, usually in the fall and spring.

Donna has fostered the success of countless others, those who have sewn the Fabulous Furs sample garments, manufactured the ready-made coats in Salyer's catalogue, and those sewing for others, using kits purchased from Salyers. She has also recently introduced ready-made coats in her catalogue.

Leather Goods

When many think of leather, they think of Harley Davidsons, and (if they're old enough!) James Dean. Leather jackets are a perennial fashion that seems to regularly return like the tide.

Dangerous Threads, the nation's largest manufacturer of leather boot harness straps, takes advantage of its Nashville location to sell customized leather wear to some of the most famous names in music. Owner **Bob Kitchener** explains that, though they contract out some of the cutting and assembly, his company customizes leather and suede jackets, skirts, bras and bustiers for the likes of Patty Loveless and Tricia Yearwood. Through his contacts in the music business, Kitchener has built up a network of clients as diverse as Travis Tritt and Garth Brooks, Z.Z. Topp and Aerosmith. "In fact," Bob says, "we had to close the retail store across from Vanderbilt University when Aerosmith came to the store." The group created quite a furor.

Their two retail stores provide the outlet for several original lines of leather clothing that Bob and **Debbie Kitchener** have developed. Working in a wholesale showroom in New York for several years gave Debbie the business know-how to manage the retail stores, and a sense of what would sell. The first store, opened in 1988, was on the second floor above a luncheonette, and they "really had to hustle to get business." However, their combined experience, and a willingness to reinvest profits back into operations, helped make Dangerous Threads a success.

Anything leather that can be embellished with rhinestones, studs, bullets, or color splicing is fair game to the Kitcheners. Their 40-70 employees manufacture boot straps and belts in the 14,000 square foot factory, but they often contract services out for special orders, such as the custom boots they made for an Alaskan hot air balloon enthusiast. He wanted his favorite balloon depicted on the side of his boots, and that's what he got. A bootmaker who often does custom work for Bob and Debbie inlaid the design on this wild footgear, in the blazing rainbow colors of the real balloon. A contractor in New York makes the bras and bustiers that Dangerous Threads turns into virtually "bulletproof" garb, with the encrusted addition of several pounds of studs and rhinestones.

"It takes a network of people for a far-ranging project like this to succeed," says Kitchener. Some of the problems of working with genuine leather and suede skins are primarily related to quality control. It is difficult, says Kitchener, to consistently find good-quality hides that match, either in color or in weight. His customers are not happy when the skirts don't quite match the tops.

Sewing Furs & Leathers

If you're interested in turning out fur or leather designs, be prepared to invest in heavy duty machines. If at first you are working with lightweight garment leather or suede, a simple straight stitch machine will do, even a domestic. However, you'll soon see the wisdom of a machine with adequate piercing power, especially where seams cross. Traditional domestic machines cannot sew heavier furs and leathers at all. In addition, there are a gamut of specialty machines for other leather processes.

Faux furs and leathers, on the other hand, are sewn easily on any machine. In fact, Donna Salyers sewed for years on her trusty Viking home machine. For top speed, though, consult an industrial sewing machine dealer for more information on faster machines.

Chapter 8

Costumes, Theatric, Fantastic and Exotic

Fantastic

Is your creative streak exceptionally wide? Is Halloween your favorite holiday, because it's a great excuse to make costumes? Then maybe exotic costumes should be your specialty. The is growing, and people who wear these incredible creations often have the imagination to dream them up, but lack the sewing skills to bring them to reality.

Potential customers are everywhere. For example, consider the Society for Creative Anachronism (SCA). Based totally in the mind, this group acts out fictional activities from the Middle Ages. Each participant chooses a character, historical, or fictional, and the player "becomes" this person. A history and résumé is developed for the character, and of course an entire wardrobe is needed.

One SCA event is a Middle Kingdom reenactment. Included in the "Middle Kingdom" is the upper middle part of the US and part of Canada. Once every six months, a fight ensues to see who can be "king" for the next half year; jousting matches and armor-clad fights with primitive weapons determine the winner. A coronation follows, complete with a historically accurate feast, with primitive utensils like 2-pronged forks and daggers instead of steak knives. Sounds a little dangerous with this group, though.) During the festivities, the participants are treated to strolling minstrels and the odd madrigal quartet or two. One observer says "It's like entering the Twilight Zone; going to one of these is a total escape from reality."

Gaining popularity, these games are played out using various and diverse scenarios. **Leah Crain** (profiled in Chapter 2) is quite active in an ongoing game that takes place on another planet, with a "Middle Earth" type terrain (as in J.R.R. Tolkein's book The Hobbit); other groups base their stories on different periods of history, or play out science fiction themes.

These events include the advancement of many different stories. A moderator controls the pace, telling the other characters where they are geographically, and at what point in the game they should take a break, etc. Movie stars and other well-known personalities are frequently present. An author speaks on a related topic, and there might be a "slave auction", to win the company of a celebrity for a few hours. A costume contest is nearly always the centerpiece of what may be a week-long event. Some of the costumes are extreme, testing the limits of fantasy.

Leah's involvement in SCA began as an adjunct to her husband Chuck's participation. Charles Crain's company makes miniature pewter figures of some of the imaginary characters. Gamers use these to advance the stories in between formal meetings. He typically maintains a booth at many of the shows.

The shows usually include seminars on costuming and characterization, and there may be fencing and belly-dancing classes, and a host of other activities. Attendance at shows usually exceeds 10,000 people, often reaching two or three times that number.

To one of these shows, Leah Crain wore a full-length, fur-trimmed wool jersey cape that she designed. Swamped with queries as to where she found it, she decided to make some up to sell from her husband's booth at his next show. A catalogue company for gaming accessories and costumes approached her to supply cloaks for their next issue. With her background sewing custom fur coats for Fabulous Furs (see previous chapter) to draw on, Crain was able to capitalize on this wonderful opportunity.

Many other groups require period costumes: Civil War reenactors, for instance. And let's not forget the Trekkies, who dress up like characters from the popular Sci-Fi series, Star Trek. Of course, not all costumes are rooted so deeply in fantasy. Some are more so: One designer creates costumes from which Pino, the famous cover artist, draws the lavish covers of romance novels.

Theatrical

Designing and creating costumes for the theater can be exciting. A local play got **Mary Bradt** involved in little theater costuming. Her whole family was in the production, and they wanted Mary to participate, too. Many years of sewing experience made costumes design a logical area for her to contribute.

In Winter Haven, Florida, not far from her home, there is the award-winning Theater Winter Haven. During the last nine years they have occasionally hired Mary for some of their costuming. The Pied Piper Players in nearby Lakeland also provide Bradt with work. Word of mouth referrals gave Mary the opportunity to sew the dance costumes for her children's' school, Harrison Arts Center High. Her close proximity to Orlando, and Disney World, is both a blessing and a curse; the theaters can turn to the many talented people there if Mary is busy.

"I'll take any kind of challenge" she says of the work that comes her way. When a problem totally stumps her, she refers to Patterns for Theatrical Costumes, a book that has several times provided a jumping off place for her designs. A "Suzy Pincushion" child's costume was satisfying to Bradt – it looked quite authentic, with a huge tomato body with green yarn, and pompons for the pin heads. Bradt says "I like it when a customer brings me a bag of fabric, with a zipper, thread, and a pattern; it's a picnic for me." Her family understands that, when she starts measuring, they won't see Mary for a while. Though "Merry Mary" likes to sew in the evenings when the house is quiet, sometimes the deadlines don't allow for such a luxury. Because her business is in her home, her two daughters chip in with cooking and other chores.

In planning stage wear, it is essential to consider how the clothing will appear from the audience. A visit by this author to the Playhouse in the Park in Cincinnati gave a glimpse into the make-believe world of costumes. An entire department is devoted to distressing clothing to appear naturally old. Color selection becomes especially important, since strong, often tinted stage lighting can sometimes wash out even deep colors. One dress, for a production about a poor backwoods family, actually was made of silk noil. The fabric was dyed and altered to look old and rustic, but held up to the repeated launderings that it withstood night after night during the play's three-week run. This kind of abuse requires that costumes be constructed with extra reinforcements, above those used in street garments. Even so, duplicate costumes are often needed, especially for the harder use of longer run plays.

Despite the fact that the audience cannot see garments close-up, stitches need to be inconspicuous for other reasons. It's vital there be no protruding loops of fabric that might catch on stage jewelry, and hems and buttons must be strong enough they don't come undone in the middle of a performance. It could be not only embarrassing, but downright dangerous for the actor. Masks must allow the person behind them to breathe, and a good line of sight can make a difference not only to the wearer, but to those on stage with him as well.

Also important in costuming for stage productions is historical accuracy. While the Playhouse in the Park keeps a wardrobe of costumes used in past stagings, designers might have to come up with the correct type of sleeve on that Elizabethan gown. If the character is supposed to be poor, too, it might be appropriate to use accessories different from those worn by other social classes. For the role of a bereaved person, it wouldn't work to clothe the actor in bright colors. Keeping to the period and mood of the setting is vital in helping the cast create the illusion of another time and place. The wrong note set by just one inaccurate detail could be enough to jar the audience back into the reality of the present.

A related option to explore is the costume needs of movie and television production companies. Commercial videography and cinematography enterprises, and corporate production departments often require costumes to reflect their logos or portray a story.

Characters

It was a Halloween costume, or rather, a pair of them, that got **Polly Trant** started in this field of dreams. She and her husband won a prize for the getups she made for a big party, which generated attention from the local mall manager. Before Polly knew it, she was making a Rainbow Brite costume for a mall promotion, and several little Sprites to go along with Ms. Brite. The next request was for Mother Goose, and a trio of reindeers for the same client. What Polly did not realize, was the mall was part of a chain of 20 such shopping meccas all over the country. Soon Polly was making costumes, including reindeers and nursery rhyme stars, to appear at malls everywhere.

Fifteen years ago, in the Texas town where Trant makes her home, a building boom led to the need for several new junior and senior high schools. Naturally, they all needed mascots, and they hired Polly to make the costumes, including their masks. She likes to make characters from pictures and photos. "Masks are just like a big stuffed animal with no stuffing," Trant says. She generally uses foam sheeting to form the shape of the head, and covers the form with fake fur. It may sound easy, but it isn't. These costumes command a higher price than those without heads. Trant has a difficult time finding anyone who is skillful enough to help with the more challenging items, so she hires help for the simpler parts of the costumes. "The people who work with me sew the feet and hands. The bodies are mostly jumpsuits, and they make those, too."

A lot of engineering goes into some of the projects. Take, for instance, a giant squirrel Trant made from the winning child's drawing of the Post Oak Mall's mascot. "Post Oak Molly" had an oversized, huge tail, which needed special support so it would not pull the rest of the costume down. A special belt and hook system Trant improvised on the spot took care of that. Another challenge she once faced was "to make a person look like a tree" for the Brazos County, Texas Crape Myrtle Festival (crape myrtle is a common shrub in the area, with deep pink flowers). Over 1,000 silk leaves and yards of hot pink bridal net helped Polly create "Magnificent Myrtle".

Another memorable assignment was to design three believable-looking recyclable products: a pile of newspapers, and a soft drink can and a plastic water bottle, both made of lamé. Most of Polly's costumes are made of fake fur, which Trant buys by the bolt. Notable among her fur creations is a goldfish used to teach swim lessons at a local pool, and serve as the spokesperson for water safety at area elementary schools. Trant's unusual business cards have photos of some of her more complicated costumes, including Chuck E. Cheese, and a beat up "Bevo" (a favorite bull-like mascot in Texas) on crutches.

A comparison with the prices in a cheerleader catalogue made Trant realize that she was seriously undercharging for her mascot creations. She got mad and increased her prices, but her customers still bought from her. "I hate to double my prices, now", she says. "But I should". She does tell her clients that if they mistreat the masks and other parts she will charge them $20 an hour to repair them. One way she is considering increasing her bottom line is by duplicating a service she has heard about, repairing and cleaning costumes. Another costume maker offers free repairs for one year; after that she cleans and repairs (fixing rips and disinfecting), for $40-50. The fake fur does require special handling, and most people don't know how to clean it.

Dance Costumes

"Dancers get thrown around a lot on stage. This just isn't something that normally happens to people in real life," says **Claudia Lynch** of Cleveland. "One theater wearing equals about ten street wearings; one ballet wearing equals 100 street wearings. At the end of a ballet, you don't want to photograph one of the tutus." Claudia should know; she was the manager of the costume shop of the Cleveland Ballet for four years.

"Sewing for ballet is much closer to couture sewing than any other kind of sewing. We couldn't do this for private clients; they just wouldn't be able to pay for it, but we use special techniques everyday for strength," in constructing the airy confections worn on stage. Although she had designed and created costumes for theaters all over the United States for ten years, Lynch felt that working with dancers was easier. "At first I thought dancers would be more difficult, but they have studied for years, and are real professionals. Dancers know their bodies; after all, they stare at them in a mirror for six to eight hours every day while they're practicing. When they tell you something about their costume fit, you'd better believe them."

Claudia says that she might also just be a rare being: an expert in making tutus. "It's sort of a lost art; a 'secret' process. You just have to figure it out on your own. It's interesting, though, to see others' work, and to see the methods they used; sometimes they duplicate something you think you've invented." Many people ask Lynch how she gets the stiff net skirts to stand up, but she says the real problem is "getting them to stand down. Their natural inclination is to stand up."

Now that Lynch has her own business, she has developed a "working method that is a cross between a costume shop and a factory". In ballet shop and in theater work, the payroll is paid with public money, or "nobody's money". If a stitcher is slow, "you hire more people, or you stay late, it's no problem. However, in my own shop, it's *my* money, and it's a problem," Lynch works hard at increasing her speed, and her bottom line. Since 1980, Claudia has done contract costume work for theaters all across the country. "Just when you think you can't stand to look at something anymore, you usually don't have to, because the job is done," she says.

When arts funding began to decline, Lynch began to branch out (See Chapter 4). Bridal work was not for her, but she has developed some other costume customers. One unusual patron is a toy soldier impersonator. His outfit required a revolving key in the back, which Claudia engineered for him. "He walks around for hours, just like a real toy soldier; you'd swear he was really mechanical!" she says. Another unusual project consisted of 60 dresses for the students of a local Irish Step Dancing (somewhat like clogging) school. In maroon wool, with a four-dart bodice, the dress has a circular skirt with box pleats in the front and on the sides. Long sleeves ending in bells at the wrist complete the silhouette. After cutting, but before assembly, the cut pieces are sent out for embellishment with a rich embroidery of white, rose and Kelly green flowers. Lynch's Sideline Design shop then picks them up for the finish work.

Exotic

Ethnic dance is the specialty of **Vicki Corona**. A dance teacher and performer, Vicki makes costumes for her dance troupe, as well as for shops and movie studios. Living in Hollywood puts her right in the middle of a hotbed of dance activity. In order to make it easy for others to make their own costumes, Corona has also written a series of booklets explaining how to cut, sew, fit and embellish many different types of dress. Because she specializes in authenticity, she sometimes even designs her own fabric, for instance, using mud painting and tapa, for Polynesian sarongs. Vicki says "I've made everything you can think of: Maori bamboo skirts, Bosnian, German, Irish, Greek, Kuwaiti dresses, Belly Dance costumes (including bra, belt, veils, skirt, harem pants, head pieces, etc.), all Polynesian type outfits, Persian, flamenco, Mexican, etc., etc. The list would go on forever."

Corona points out an interesting fact about dance dress: "You can tell what any ethnic dance will look like when you see the costumes. For example, Irish dances use just the feet, so there's that pleated skirt for both men and women. But they never use arms or hand gestures, so there's a *very* tight, form-fitting jacket on top. Kimono are highly restrictive, and so Japanese dance is very reserved. This analysis holds true for every single cultural dance."

There are more exotic costume needs for other classes of dancers: dance teams, football cheerleaders, Vegas showgirls, and stripteasers of both sexes. The male dancers used for "bachelorette" parties need to have someone make those easy-off Velcro numbers! Show choirs need new costumes periodically. Schools are usually not willing to pay well, and the lead time is probably going to be so short that you will tear your hair out. You may choose to make them anyway: it could be a great way to sew for a large variety of bodies and learn about sewing under fire.

Be aware that some costume shops and their clients have contracts with unions. This can be troublesome if you don't take it into account. Be sure you understand ahead of time the expectations in your contract, in order to comply with union rules. When Claudia Lynch made many of the costumes for the Cincinnati Ballet Company's premiere of *Peter Pan*, she was forced to sew off premises because of union rules. This was inconvenient for her because she had to find another place in the city to sew. Her own shop was nearly 250 miles away in Cleveland. In most union productions, wardrobe people maintain the costumes from the final fittings on.

Chapter 9

Kid Stuff: Children's Clothing

Custom Children's Clothing

A talent for creating a fresh, whimsical look in children's clothes can springboard to a business specializing in making munchkinwear. That's just what **Margaret Marinucci** calls her business. "My custom clothing business, Munchkinwear by Marinucci, is in its infancy (no pun intended)" she says. "I've been an 'at-home mom' for the past 6+ years, and am hoping to have a solid business established by the time my 2-year old is in first grade." Margaret has been making childrenswear for specialty shops and on a special-order basis. "I love to sew and dress my three girls in coordinating outfits. 'Munchkins' developed when people kept asking where I bought the clothes."

Margaret believes her strong suit is customer service. She's convinced the personal service aspect of her business is what keeps many of her customers coming back; Marinucci feels "it's a status thing with them". However, she has other strengths, too, including significant business experience. She worked for 10 years for a large direct writer insurance company, as the head of a 35-person department. The responsibility of a $12 million budget gave her a background in making a business work. Of course, she's dealing with a much smaller budget for now.

With only word of mouth advertising, Margaret has experienced as much as an eight month backlog of orders. She says her steady clients know she needs leeway to fill their orders, and some of them will help her out when she's ready to expand. The best part is that the kids' clothing has helped her expand into other areas, a fact that helps "fill in the gaps" of the seasonal nature of creating for children. (See Chapter 16 for more.)

Quantity Sewing

Marji Ross of Cincinnati has taken this concept a giant step further. With an idea for an appliquéd, reversible children's' jumper and shortall, Marji made some samples and took them to a retail buyer. They were well received, and her business was on its way. She now has several accounts, mostly upscale consignment-type shops.

For the production work required to provide dozens of the same item, Marji finds using a variety of industrial machines and techniques essential. She "chain" sows, repeating the same seam over and over without cutting the thread until all the pieces are sewn. This industrial trick alone saves Ross countless hours a year, which is vitally important to maximizing her profits. She has no employees, so every moment saved helps.

Preemie Wear

Yet another entrepreneur who has found a niche in the childrenswear market is **Cindi Leslie** of Michigan. She was working as an accountant for KMart, but decided she wanted to work at home while her four children were small. "I wanted to sew as a business, but I didn't want to get involved in making different sizes," she says. "Also, toddler wear is very competitive, and I didn't want to feel torn about sewing for my own kids." She has never herself had a premature baby, but she noticed that it was next to impossible to find serviceable garments for "preemies". Cindi decided to test a few garments to see if they would sell. She was pleasantly surprised by their reception.

At first, Leslie called on and sold to area resale and consignment stores. With photos, drawings, samples and fabric swatches, she could take orders easily. One store owner was very helpful, giving Cindi suggestions on what would sell best. In her situation, selling her products to these non-traditional stores was better than selling to retail, because she could not meet the scale of production necessary for retail sales. Nor was Cindi ready for such a time commitment, or the pressures of deadlines and recordkeeping. Supplying a total of eleven stores, only one of them retail, she felt she could easily keep up with the demand for new product. After an initial personal contact with the stores, sending order forms and swatches generates subsequent sales.

When she was ready to expand her business, Leslie sent out flyers to new stores. She has long advertised in a publication directed to the mothers of twins, "Mothers of Multiples". Leslie has also investigated the cost of advertising in a local free paper serving the entire Detroit Metro area, and largely targeted to parents. Another vehicle Leslie is considering is a marketing product called "Stork Bonds", which includes package of freebies and service advertising given to each new parent at area hospitals. Leaving her business cards at the offices of area obstetricians is yet another way for her to advertise her products. To find out which advertising method works best, Leslie always asks how customers found out about her. So far, word of mouth has been especially helpful. Because preemies grow rapidly, there isn't much repeat business built into Early Arrivals, Leslie's company, but she feels her superior product will stand on its own merit.

Leslie buys wholesale 4-6 bolts of one fabric at a time, usually 50/50 poly/cotton interlock. This fiber combination washes better than 100% cotton, and is still soft enough for an infant's tender skin. The garments are serged together, using a soft nylon thread, except on details such as bunting zippers and topstitching. Early Arrivals offers an array of choices: buntings for winter, gown sleepers, and 2-piece outfits for either boys or girls. Holiday seasons offer more festive styles and fabrications. With each garment, Leslie includes a matching cap, a vital addition to the comfort and health of a premature infant. Buying wholesale also allows Cindi to remain competitive, yet still make a profit.

Since Leslie is selling her products as a business, each of her garments includes a care and content label. Strict federal laws govern this issue, and it is wise to investigate the latest rulings about labeling before attempting to sell your designs. Contact your local extension service or Small Business Administration office for more information.

Cindi Leslie recommends two magazines for style and fabric news: *Kid's Fashion Magazine* and *Children's Business*. She also uses *Sourcing News*, from T.I.P., for fabric sourcing. See Sources. Regional fabric shows can be invaluable for making contacts and finding resources for wholesale fabric purchases.

PART TWO:

Home Furnishings

↳ Upholstery & Slipcovers

↳ Draperies & Window Treatments

↳ Home Decoration Accessories

Chapter 10

Upholstery & Slipcovers

Many of the same people who balk at paying a dressmaker a living wage for her services, will spend a small fortune on their homes without blinking an eye. Because of the perceived complexity of most upholstery and slipcovering projects, do-it-yourselfers often feel too intimidated to tackle them, and willingly pay someone else to do the job. The entrepreneur who wants to make a higher markup on sewing might want to tap into this market.

Slipcovers

To help others start businesses in slipcovering, **Theresa Lindal** and **Mary Bailey** put together a series of educational videos. They then began selling them at trade shows in conjunction with their excellent seminars. Partners for several years in their own drapery and home dec workroom before they decided to take their show on the road, Theresa and Mary had independently sewn for others before that.

When Theresa Lindal first moved to the Traverse Bay area, she began sewing for a decorator workroom. Unfortunately, the owner of the shop was just dabbling in the business, as a hobby, while Theresa had a more robust business in mind. She had been to a few trade shows, and they inspired her to go into business on her own. In addition to making the slipcovers and draperies, she also sold fabric. "I liked helping pick out fabric and styles, and then creating what I designed," she says. Unless they were "real tricky", Lindal also did her own installations. In about 1985, when her former employer retired, Lindal acquired the decorator workroom business, and she moved the business to a building adjacent to her home.

In 1980, Lindal had met Mary Bailey, who had made slipcovers exclusively for 17 years. They worked together for a while part-time, and eventually the two formed T&M Creations, in addition to each of their workroom businesses. They collaborated on teaching others what Lindal describes as the "lost art" of slipcover making. "Slipcovers are ecologically sound, and economically sound, too", says Lindal. "Unfortunately, the books written about them are sometimes hard to understand."

The partners thought about making a video for some time. Then they saw a video on making draperies, and Theresa says "I thought 'uh-oh, we'd better get busy'". In 1989, they produced their first, basic 94-minute slipcovering video through a local videography company. The next year, they followed that effort with four more one-hour videos: a more in-depth look at slipcovers, two videos on cushions (an integral part of a slipcover), and one on how to make pinch-pleated draperies. (See Chapter 25 for more on videos).

Transcontinental Odyssey

Kathleen Amburgy's first slipcovering project was for a friend, who talked her into covering a Queen Anne chair for her; the friend already had fabric, and wasn't too particular about the way it would turn out. However, it turned out beautifully, and Kathleen, who had been doing dressmaking up to then, (under)charged her the princely sum of $6.50. Some years later, after the cover had faded, the friend asked Kathleen to cover it again, and would she again charge $6.50? Amburgy said she certainly would take on the project, but she certainly would - and did - charge much more this time.

Kathleen grew up in England, and was taught to sew as a matter of course. She had a fierce desire to "someday have a shop". Though her father maintained she should "Stay home and let your mother learn you to sew", she applied to, and was accepted by the Bloomsbury Technical School, despite being a year underage. Three months into her first term, the war caused the school to evacuate London and move to Hertfordshire, where classes continued. Bloomsbury was run strictly like any English school, and the girls' training was on clothing for wealthy Londoners. The girls in the school did not see the fittings done. Nevertheless, they were expected to make the garments to perfection, sometimes taking as long as three months to finish one item. In addition to their dressmaking class, during their eight hour day students worked in one of four other required courses: Millinery, Photography, Tailoring or Corset Making!

From this school, Amburgy was placed at Peter Robinson, a dressmaking establishment in Berkeley Square in London, for a three-year apprenticeship. Peter Robinson catered to not only the well-to-do in the surrounding neighborhood, but to the Royal Family, as well. For Kathleen, this was sheer heaven. She was always the youngest, so she had to be the "tea girl", preparing the afternoon tea, and taking messages to the tailors. Since all the gentlemen wore tails, there was a very formal atmosphere that charged young Kathleen with excitement. A Frenchwoman, "Madame", was in charge of the dressmakers, and there were six mannequins, or models, to be admired. To a young girl, these gorgeous models draping chiffon scarves over their coiffures between changes were the ultimate in glamour and sophistication. Kathleen assures us "there was no messing around". It was hard work, and she had a long train or bus ride each way from her home. In addition, she only earned 25 shillings (about $5) per week for her labors. After all, she was an apprentice, learning her trade.

An uncle, an excellent tailor, often teased Kathleen that she would marry a tailor like himself, but that was not to be. In 1947, she came to the US as a war bride to "a tiny farm in the middle of nowhere in Ohio". This contrast to her very cosmopolitan life in England made her feel "like a pioneer woman". Kathleen, who had never been around farm animals, was now milking cows on a farm with no electricity. Life was very hard for many years, during which Kathleen had to make do with her treadle Singer. When they moved to Cincinnati, she "got a good electric sewing machine" (notice that she didn't say "electric *lights*"). Eventually, she came to support herself and her five children using this machine.

Now living in Lebanon, Ohio, and happily remarried, Kathleen operates the Amburgy Sewing Shoppe out of her garage, family room, and other rooms in her home that she has taken over and remodeled for business. Advertising only for the first three weeks after she moved there, she quickly built a strong business. She draws faithful customers from as far as forty miles away. A big workspace in the garage, well insulated from the cold, provides the room needed for making slipcovers and drapes, and keeps the mess out of the rest of the house. Two large tables and several industrial machines help Amburgy to fill orders.

Upholstery

Upholstery requires some sewing, but often uses stapling more than stitching. Cushion seams require joining on a sewing machine, and many upholsterers keep a stitcher on staff for that purpose, or have a reliable freelancer. Through her experience in calling around and asking for an apprentice job, **Wendy Rainbolt** says "it seemed female upholsterers are frowned upon". Wendy, who does both slipcovering and upholstery from her studio in Allen, Texas, says slipcovers are back in style these days. Many people prefer the ease of changing their decor, and the convenience of cleaning. Also, with recovering, the unit must be "torn down", which is a big job, so slipcovers are much easier, and if skillfully done, the furniture can look upholstered.

"Sewing for someone is a very personal thing", Rainbolt says. "The customer has picked out fabric and a style to put in their home to express themselves." Wendy feels that, as an extension of the customer's taste, she has a responsibility to do the best she can. She's been successful in developing good relationships with many customers who keep coming back to her for more work. "They call me to reupholster a chair, and after a year or so, they find other things they want me to do. I work my way through their entire home. I didn't expect this, but I guess these people like the customer service and attention I give them".

Though her customers sometimes supply the fabric, Rainbolt has fabric books to flip through for color choices. When the client asks for "burnt orange", Wendy can turn to a sample and ask "Is this burnt orange, do we agree?" This keeps disagreements to a minimum. As an added service Wendy sometimes picks up swatches to show her customer. "I want to be a distant family relative", she says. "I hold their hands" when they need extra assistance. Eventually, she may charge for the time this takes, but for now she feels the learning experience is worth her time. She is building credibility, and it seems to be working well; clients who were at first unsure seem reassured by her willingness to come by and measure for an estimate. "My customer profile is that of an older female, either a businesswoman, or retired." On prices, Rainbolt says "You must charge what you need to charge." This was the hardest part for her in the beginning, "because it's hard to feel worth the price you're charging." Also, working with a decorator reduces the gross profit margin, as the decorator then marks up the upholsterer's service by doubling (or more) the price to the client, so your prices need to reflect that.

A friend with a minivan helps Rainbolt pick up and deliver the larger pieces, but she hauls the smaller ones in her hatchback. At first, she thought people would not accept her driving up in a car to pick up their furniture, but it hasn't been a problem. Though she doesn't charge a pickup fee for the smaller pieces, if her friend helps her, she charges the customer by the mile. Her clients also have the option of dropping pieces at her home. Once the furniture is there, a large table on sawhorses doubles as a cutting table and a worktable for fitting. Other essential tools for upholstery include a heavy duty sewing machine, stretchers, hammers, clamps, tack lifters, and other hardware-type items.

Some of the needs and materials of upholstery are the same as for making slipcovers, but there are differences, as well. According to **Mary Bailey**, of T&M Creations, the paper-cored piping used in upholstery will disintegrate during the cleaning process used for a slipcover. A washable cotton or polyester cording should be used. Also, there is no need for zippers in upholstery, but they are an absolute necessity for slipcovers. The tearing down process of reupholstery creates a problem of what to do with the resultant debris. Old fabric, horsehair and foam, as well as used tacks, and other sharp objects can be difficult to dispose. Both types of furniture renewal require foam sculpting for the cushions, so be aware that this makes a mess too. ("This is when you finally get to use that electric knife that's been in your kitchen drawer for years," says Theresa Lindal.) An upholsterer usually has a shop, while slipcovers can often be sewn from a private home, depending on your zoning requirements.

Chairs and sofas are only part of the upholstery story. There are other items that need to be repaired and recovered as well. Auto, boat and airplane interiors, and motorcycle and tractor seats are oft-requested recovering jobs. (See Chapter 21 for more on this specialty.) One company in northern Michigan has won trophies in regional car shows for their work in custom upholstery for antique cars.

Chapter 11

Draperies & Window Treatments

A current trend in new homes places very large windows in almost every room. This represents an a potentially huge expense for the homeowner - and a wonderful opportunity for the window specialist. Often, specialists can create sales by suggesting top treatments, rather than expensive draperies from a department store. This may cost less for the client.

"To the Trade": Working with Designers

Working with a decorator is one avenue for referral business. This relationship often flourishes due to mutual need, and can be extremely lucrative for the drapery or window specialist, who can spend more of her time sewing, and less selling. However, there can be a drawback to this arrangement. In order to be competitive, the drapery workroom must often shave its prices thin to allow for the markup the decorator will charge. If the final cost to the client becomes too high the decorator may choose to use a different workroom, or lose the account altogether.

One way workrooms add profit to their price structure is to markup the fabric they sell. **Cindy Purdy**, of Union, Kentucky, says she will work on fabric provided by the customer, because she tries to give her customers breaks whenever she can. New to this area, Cindy has had a rough time finding out what other workrooms charge. Access to this information would help her keep her prices competitive: not so low that she can't keep up with the work; not so high that she is pricing herself out of the market. "No one wants to tell you what they charge," she says. "I've tried calling other workrooms, and they simply won't share their base price, unless I convince them I'm a decorator. The problem is they charge a decorator one price, and the general public another." Purdy feels this hurts the small workroom; she doesn't mind sharing her prices with other window specialists because "there are so many variables in custom work; you just need a place to start". She suspects that calls for ads she has run for her services are sometimes from other aspiring window treatment specialists. "Most people don't know that in drapery work you charge by the number of widths of material. $15 per width, for example, includes cutting, measuring, hems, yardage, and pleating, in addition to the cost of the fabric." Purdy has sample books, and though she doesn't require her clients to purchase fabric from her, when they do she uses a regular "keystone" markup (double the wholesale price), then discounts 20% from there.

Purdy has been sewing since high school, but didn't realize she had a marketable skill until she worked in a drapery workroom for someone else. Encouraged by a local women's group to get business cards printed and go out on her own, Cindy mustered the courage to break out of her normal "introverted" self to become self-employed. Beyond her initial trips to the local fabric stores to leave business cards, most of her business has come from word-of-mouth advertising. Often, people who know what they want but can't sew call her. "They usually say 'this is real easy; I don't think it will take too long'" Purdy says. She has learned to see through these calls, and take charge of the situation better. Her best marketing efforts have come from her college-age daughter, who "tells everyone what her mom does", and has helped Cindy computerize her price lists. Purdy's husband comes in handy, too, for cutting the cornice boards for some of her more complicated jobs. Though Cindy feels she lacks marketing skills and doesn't expect to "get rich" in this business, she finds the work very satisfying, especially the creative part of it.

Retail Workroom

Every time her family moved with her husband's job, **Dawn Haugom** sewed fresh window treatments for their new home. Inevitably, the neighbors would start asking her to help with their redecorating efforts. Soon her sewing business consumed more time and energy than Dawn spent at her high school teaching position. When husband Bob's company sent him to Cincinnati, Dawn decided not to look for another teaching job, and instead opened Window Fashions from her home. Through "quality work and exceptional service", word spread and the business grew.

A visit to Haugom's workroom illustrates the space required for making window treatments. It takes up over half of her very large basement, where she has all the equipment of a much larger workroom. Two large cutting tables, a swag maker, and three industrial machine stations, plus other accessories consume most of the floor space in her work area, which is easily accessible, but separate, from the rest of her home. Good lighting overhead and white-painted walls ensure that Dawn and an assistant have ample light for sewing and measuring. Most of Haugom's customer contact occurs in the customers' homes, so she rarely has visitors to this area.

Specializing in window treatments and bed coverings, Haugom decided that investment in a large table would be a good idea. Her first one is still in use, one that Dawn "put together myself". It is wood, eight feet long by four feet wide, with below that a shelf that stores the customer's fabric while it awaits transition into draperies. A padded canvas top allows the long lengths of fabric to be pressed in place. This reduces movement of the yardage, and prevents false measurements. Since the table is so large, an electrical outlet was installed overhead for an iron. This keeps extension cords out of the way. Some workrooms have a sliding electrical outlet arrangement above the work tables, which permits free movement of the iron and cord.

With the addition of her Sizemaster table, Dawn can now accurately measure draperies up to twelve feet long by five feet wide. This excellent tool is very nearly the same size as her older one, but has a handy set of aluminum edge rules and a hem clamp, indispensable for making sure each panel of a set of draperies is the same size. A zero-line on the marked surface makes it easy to "table out" – to smooth the fabric onto the table preparatory to cutting. At the end of the table is a dual bolt holder; one holds lining fabric at all times, the other holds the fashion fabric. This allows for accurate measuring. Dawn can pull identical lengths of both the lining and the fashion fabric out at the same time. Another sensible investment for Haugom was a Dofix boiler steam iron, whose tank provides ample steam for pressing the fabric for a multitude of window dressings.

Haugom recommends anyone interested in operating a drapery workroom keep up-to-date on fashion trends in home decorating. A wonderful way of staying current is attending the trade shows put on by publishers of various trade magazines. They usually have seminars on techniques and trends and how to create the hottest looks. In addition, suppliers and manufacturers showcase their latest products, to help specialists provide a true professional edge.

For instance, Dawn Haugom relies on the Swagmaster she researched at a trade show to make a popular top treatment. This handy tool helps her instantly measure and drape a swag, normally not a precise process without a pattern drawn specifically for each window. Though the Swagmaster takes up an area of about 4 feet by 6 feet, it saves countless hours of measuring, especially when a job involves a number of windows needing similar treatments. Once the size and number of drapes are set, an identical swag can be made over and over.

Learning to use a Skilsaw has also been a boon to Dawn. Many window treatments also require custom cornice boards and other wooden hardware. With the Skilsaw, Dawn can cut and assemble them in her workroom, providing yet another edge over her competitors.

Though she used to install finished treatments herself, Haugom now employs an installer who works on an hourly basis by appointment. This frees Dawn from climbing ladders and getting grubby in the middle of a selling day, and lets her plan larger blocks of sewing time in her workroom.

From Basement to Storefront

A move to North Carolina from her Florida home in 1972 spurred **Lois Wernicke** to look around for something to do. She decided to start a drapery business in her basement, and purchases the three basic machines: a serger, a commercial sewing machine and a blindstitch machine. By 1975, she was so busy that when she learned that her daughter, **Cheryl Strickland**, was moving to town, she pleaded "Whatever you do, when you get here, just help me get caught up for two weeks". Cheryl says "We must have never gotten caught up, because I stayed with Mom for 15 years." All the company's window treatments became Cheryl's responsibility.

For about twelve years, Drapery Arts stayed in Lois's basement, where it grew and grew. "Working in my parent's home was a perfect solution for me in my child rearing years," says Cheryl. "At one time, there were twelve people in the basement, with two of us pregnant." It was a little cramped. "We were always blessed with wonderful employees, though. Part of our success was that we didn't treat them like employees; we didn't even call them employees, and we said that they worked with us, rather than for us. We encouraged their input, and some of them had very good, time-saving ideas. They were also given a bonus for their ideas. We tried to use the Golden Rule in our business." Apparently, the workers appreciated this, as several stayed with Drapery Arts for more than ten years.

The business continued to grow when Cheryl's sister, **Betty Lasseter**, also moved to town and joined the company. They opened a sales office, renamed the company Drapery Arts and Interiors, and Betty took over the sales and design responsibilities. Lois was in charge of special treatments and installations, and Cheryl took over the production scheduling, the people managing, and all the bookkeeping. "We each had the area of responsibility where we got the most joy," Cheryl says. She found that she enjoyed the management end the most – some people don't, and would be very unhappy if that's all they did. "Though it isn't always possible in a small business, you should do what you like, if you can. Our arrangement worked beautifully, and no one coveted anyone else's job; we meshed well."

As they grew, Betty found a property on the main highway in town, and put a bid on it. With their excellent credit they had no problem getting a loan from the bank, and they moved aboveground to a showroom and sales floor, with an attached 2,000 square foot workroom in back. Many customers who relied on them for design requested wallpaper to match their fabric, so they ended up carrying nearly as many wallpaper books as fabric swatchbooks. Their slogan "We do it all, from design to install", told the story of how their business fit in the local market.

Their business had grown, incredibly, without ever having a Yellow Pages ad. Part of their success had come from development of several wholesale workroom accounts. A representative of the local Ethan Allen retail furniture store approached them and said "We've seen your work, and we consider you the best workroom in western North Carolina. Would you be interested in doing our sewing?" Lois and her daughters thought about this, asking themselves how they would feel about their gorgeous work going out under someone else's name. They felt is was a big responsibility to do work this way, and decided to try it for a while. They followed certain guidelines in their wholesale work: they would do the same quality of work for others that they did for their own customers, and they would never tell anyone that they did work for the retailer. Because the furniture store was marking up their prices, it was more expensive for the customer to buy from Ethan Allen. Many times, both companies were bidding on the same job. Respecting the store's business, and being discreet about the working arrangement with them led to many referrals from Ethan Allen. Eventually, Strickland's company had more than forty wholesale accounts.

The heavy volume produced by so many wholesale accounts, coupled with their regular retail business, at times required over 21 employees. Today, Strickland says she would think twice about having this kind of responsibility. "With all the federal mandates and lawsuits, and the health insurance problem, it would be too worrisome." She doesn't have these worries anymore.

Meanwhile, Betty Lasseter left the company to focus on broader design services, "from the trees outside, to floor plans". One day, when listening to some of her designers talk with great excitement about an upcoming project, Cheryl realized she didn't share their enthusiasm. She was ready to look beyond the business she had helped her mother build. In addition, Lois wanted to retire to Florida, so they sold the business.

Shifting Focus

Working with outside decorators for many years had convinced Strickland of the incredible need for technical training in her field. Although many of the decorators had advanced degrees in interior design, they called on her for measuring and yardage calculations all the time. One such designer called the most: a professor in the subject at a local college who has a Masters in Interior Design. Interior design grads hired for Drapery Arts and Interiors needed training from scratch, as if they knew nothing, just for the basic information they needed to work in this area. Seeing this lack of such basic skills convinced Cheryl that someone should develop a training program.

After selling the company, Strickland called many of her former wholesale clients and asked them if they were interested in a seminar for their employees. All of them showed an enthusiastic and positive interest, so Cheryl decided to teach. The first thing she wanted to do was to write something to give her students. Two nights every week she went to the library to work on an outline-based handbook. With this accomplished, she sent out flyers advertising her first seminar in nearby Asheville. Fifty people attended, and Cheryl made $600. The best part of the evening came when a design student approached her at the break to let Cheryl know how much she was learning and how much she was enjoying the program. "When I thanked her and told her how much I appreciated her comments because it was my first effort, her jaw dropped open. She couldn't believe this was my first time. That made my day, and gave me the confidence to keep going." A self-described "closet actress and comedienne", Strickland strives to make the program enjoyable, entertaining as well as educational.

From then on, seeking to make professional speaking her new career, Cheryl pointed out to the organizers of a trade show that there was nothing on their program with technical information. They asked her to send them something, which turned out to be the handbook she had developed. In a short time, they called and agreed with her that her ideas would be welcomed by their audience, and hired her to speak at two sessions at an upcoming show. "I taught 500 people at that show, and received across the board 100% 'excellent' evaluation ratings. They have hired me for every show since."

The next important step in her career path was writing for a trade magazine, though Cheryl didn't realize exactly what she was getting into at the time. She called the editor of *Draperies & Window Coverings (D&WC)* and made arrangements to meet with her at the next show the magazine was sponsoring. At this meeting, Strickland pointed out that she thought their readers would like to read about the same subjects covered in her seminar. The editor said "Cheryl, we will print anything you want to write." On her way out, Strickland said to herself: "Well, now you've got a job, you'd better learn to write!". So it was back to the library, this time for books on writing. Since then, she's written something for the publication every month. Her biography at the end of each article includes the information about her seminars, which is good advertising, and has generated a great deal of business. "I write the articles the way I teach my classes," she says. "Step by step, they progress towards more difficult processes." In 1991, she was featured on the cover of *D&WC* magazine and a profile of her business was the lead story. "There were pictures of us working in Mom's basement," she says.

Strickland's good relationship with *D&WC* helped when she wrote her first book, *A Practical Guide to Soft Window Coverings*. Clark Publishing, who publishes the magazine, also published Cheryl's book, and continues to advertise it in *D&WC*. Volume Two, with more difficult treatments, design ideas, and bed treatment information, is in the works. It's behind schedule at this writing; "I have so many seminar dates, I can't get it finished", says Strickland. A Designer's Sketch Pad that she invented is another good seller for Cheryl. With sixty different window treatment designs illustrated, this handy little pad makes the process of communication between designer and client easier. The onionskin paper allows tracing or photocopying of designs for reproduction in a customer's file, or attachment to the job ticket. She sells these, along with her book, at the trade shows sponsored and attended by *D&WC*, including the World of Window Coverings show, usually held in the spring somewhere on the East Coast.

Strickland also publishes a monthly newsletter, *Sew WHAT?,* which addresses many concerns of drapery workrooms. Each issue includes patterns and tips for treatments, resource information, and an industry calendar. Recently, Cheryl built a classroom facility to hold her new Professional Drapery Workroom School.

Getting Started

A fan of Cheryl Strickland's seminars is Cincinnatian **Bette Dean**. She says "Cheryl gives you really good ideas; she has all sorts of neat concepts on covering Palladium windows, as well as arches, and other shapes." Dean had been a travel agent when the Gulf War broke out and caused the travel business to fizzle. She was worried about company layoffs. One weekend, she went to a window treatment seminar at a local conference center, just for something to do. While sitting in the class she realized she could make window treatments as a business.

In preparation, Dean took an Interior Design class at her local adult education center. It gave her wonderful knowledge of using color, coordinating prints, and creating focal points. It also helped her understand what fabric goes with what furniture. "You can't put Priscilla curtains with contemporary furniture," she says. Getting feedback from the customer is important to determine their lifestyle, an important consideration in making choices on interior design. Dean also invested in books on how to do various treatments, and when the fabric store had them on sale for $2 apiece, she invested in every pattern for window treatments available.

Bette went to the local new home show and took photos of windows in the beautifully decorated show houses. She added these to a book that contains magazine pictures, which she uses to present ideas to customers and to get feedback on what they want. Later, as she made new treatments, she took photos of each job.

Supplies and Machines

Finding wholesale suppliers has helped Bette. For example, in three years, she uses about 500 yards of drapery lining, so she buys it in 100-yard bolts. "You don't want to buy a package of plastic rings; you want to buy in lots of 1,000," she recommends. Dean buys zippers by the 100-yard roll. Cording is another item stockpiled in bulk, and in various sizes. Dean adds "It's much easier to work efficiently when you're not constantly stopping to run out and get a bit of this or that to finish a project."

The machines you use in your drapery business should be able to handle long stretches of fabric for hours at a time. An industrial blindstitch machine for hemming is an absolute must; once you've hemmed several pairs of drapes at once with one of these speed demons, you'll never go back to a domestic machine. For curtains with ruffled trim, a Johnson Ruffling Machine might come in handy ; a special calibration on this machine allows the precise gathering ratio needed for such work.

Stage Curtains

A seldom considered niche in draperies and window treatments is manufacturing stage curtains. **Sue Zimmerman**, of Minneapolis, is an expert in this. She works as the theater draping specialist for Gopher Stage Lighting, Inc. Though she doesn't have guaranteed hours, she can make her own schedule as long as the jobs are finished on time. Up until recently, Sue was the only stitcher Gopher employed; she's had to train someone else to help.

Because a set of theater curtains lasts about 15-20 years, there is a limited market. However, as Sue points out, school districts often replace all the curtains in their schools at once, creating large, profitable jobs. Colleges and universities, and regular theaters are also customers, both for replacement curtains, and new ones. Public schools are obligated to advertise for bids, which is how Zimmerman's employer gets the jobs.

Sue works with a Chandler Walking Foot machine mounted to a large, 10' by 10' table. Because some of the grand drapes are as large as 20' high by 30' wide per side, an enormous cutting area is a must.

A 6' by 24' table with a bolt holder at one end for the fabric (like a paper towel holder, according to Zimmerman), makes the cutting easier. There may be as many as 15 cuts of fabric per side of each drape. "Making these curtains is easy," she says. "The hard part is heaving the material around."

The main fabric used in theater curtains is 100% cotton woven velour, commonly in the 25 ounce weight. Because it's required that stage curtain fabric be firetreated, this process is done at the mill, along with the dyeing. Some theaters request rep cloth, which has a herringbone weave, and others might choose a cheaper alternative: Commando cloth, a heavy chamois-like cloth. Lining is made of Ranger cloth, a heavy broadcloth, usually black. Most front curtains are colored deep red, blue, green or black, and the back curtains are most often made of a black, 20 ounce version of the velour.

Gopher Stage Lighting also makes muslin backdrops, usually natural or sky blue, and scrim, which is either white or black. Because the scrim fabric is a fine cotton net, it is unstable in the weave and difficult to cut and handle. Sewing this slippery stuff costs more than other kinds of fabric. However, it is manufactured in widths from 9-40', so it doesn't need much done to it – just top, bottom and side seams.

Theater curtains, on the other hand, require a lot of sewing. They are generally box pleated, which can cause a tug of war at the machine. "Sewing the 32 ounce fabric is like trying to sew a small rug, it's so thick," says Sue. She uses 1 1/2" wide seams, and a 3 1/2" wide hemp webbing in the top pleats. Muslin pockets for the chain weight that keeps the curtain along the floor finish the hems. To prevent undue wear, the chain is suspended in the pocket, then attached at either end. A heavy nylon thread is used to sew the drapes, with a stitch almost 1/4" long to accommodate the thickness of the fabric.

Most theater curtain sewing is straight forward. However, some fancy gold Austrian shade style curtains were a design challenge for Zimmerman. She made her own 3" wide tape, then added 2" wide "D" rings. Sue first seamed two widths of fabric, then added the tapes and rings to each pair of widths, to make each swag. She's hoping for encores!

Chapter 12

Home Decoration Accessories

Accessories for a room, like accessories for a clothing ensemble, can make or break the decorating scheme. Padded valances, table skirts, headboards, dust ruffles and other bedroom coordinates, bath linens (including shower curtains and embellished towels), and countless other home accessories offer areas for specialization. Those fabric stores that cater to the home dec market often need stitchers to whom to refer their customers who either don't sew, or do not have the self-confidence to tackle such large projects.

Cushions

Some drapery workrooms also furnish the labor for decorative pillows and bedcoverings, and many upholsterers and slipcover makers also sew custom cushions.

Taking a chair to an upholstery class every week, **Mary Beth Dimmock** impressed her instructor so much that he hired her to make cushions in his Pittsburgh shop. Subsequent jobs at other workrooms added to Mary Beth's knowledge. Moving to Denver, she utilized this education and began a part-time business specializing in sewing cushions for upholsterers.

After she had been sewing cushions in Denver for several years, one of her clients referred the Vail Hyatt Hotel Beavercreek to her; they needed 30 bedspreads and shams for the guest rooms. They asked Dimmock for an estimate, so she went to Vail to spend a night in the hotel. Understandably, she didn't sleep well that night. She worried about what to charge them for the work. She gave them what she thought might be a high dollar estimate. "The customer didn't bat an eye", she says. "I figured that by the time I paid someone to quilt the tops, I could buy the quilting machine, so I bought a Nolting, and did that part of it myself". (see Chapter 17 for more information on quilting.)

Mary Beth not only found the hotel job profitable, she found eliminating the middleman more beneficial. While working for the upholsterers, she had to keep her prices low, so *they* could charge a markup. In addition, most cushions are so basic there isn't much opportunity to charge higher prices.

Dimmock orders her foam through a wholesale upholstery supply house. Zippers are bought by the roll. Mary Beth says zippers in upholstered furniture are really for the convenience of the upholsterer, rather than for cleaning the cushions later. Though she doesn't ordinarily sell fabric to her clients, she uses her connections with the wholesale house to procure batting, lining fabrics and notions. Since she likes the sewing part better than the sheer physical labor of upholstery, Dimmock prefers making the cushions. "It's been a learning experience," she says. For instance, sewing cording so the stitching didn't show came from working at it over and over until it finally occurred to her to offset the first stitching 1/8 of an inch. Then the second row of stitching could be closer to the cording, hiding the first.

Smaller Accessories

Billing her wares as "useful household items", **Lil Van Cise** has made a part-time business of sewing home dec items while moonlighting from her full-time job with the Nuclear Regulatory Commission. Preparing to retire in a few years, Van Cise is building a business, and spends 30 hours a week doing so. Although she does sell many of her products at crafts shows, they are more upscale than the run of the mill craft item (also see Chapter 14). Table linens, throw pillows, "Quillows" (pillows which open out to become quilts), kitchen articles and holiday-related decorative accessories are just some of the items that Van Cise makes and sells.

In 1992, Lil made enough product to take to a half dozen Christmas shows. She sold 30 Christmas tree skirts alone, plus took special orders for several others. Because she likes to get the input of her customers, Lil enjoys the face-to-face contact of craft shows and custom work. "It's helpful to know how people are using my items," she says. "and I get to see what the market is and what it will bear. I want to satisfy my customers; it must be working – I haven't had many complaints."

A year-round basic for Van Cise is custom baby quilts. These in turn often lead to the purchase of other coordinating special order items. Table runners and placemats, with matching tablecloths and napkins, are popular choices, and a favorite of Van Cise. Her best-selling product is a kitchen towel with a potholder as the handle, which buttons to a kitchen drawer pull. It's the cheapest thing she sells, and she makes hundreds. "They're good for gifts, and very useful" she explains.

To maximize profits, Van Cise buys most of her fabrics wholesale. She often goes to the library, finds a source for a fabric that interests her, and writes to the company asking for a list of wholesale dealers. She uses two large wholesale houses in particular, and has established accounts with them. One wholesale company requires that she send payment by check, after which they send her order. Her special threads are purchased directly from the company in bulk; occasionally, she runs into her local fabric store for smaller amounts. In order to be prepared for when she has sewing time available, Van Cise keeps plenty on hand to work with. She also switches projects frequently so that she doesn't tire of making the same thing over and over. For maximum efficiency, she keeps sergers set up for rolled hems (she does many on her table linens), one with light thread, the other with dark. This changes to red and green thread when it's time to make Christmas items. Fortunately, her family and friends help her out. One family member gets the wooden parts for some of her craft items for her, and her "significant other" does a big part of the fabric research, filing and correspondence. This must be very helpful to someone who already works 70 hours a week!

PART THREE:

PARAPHERNALIA

↳ Handmade Specialty Items

↳ Craft & Boutique Items

↳ Banners & Flags

↳ Dolls, Puppets & Toys

↳ Hand & Machine Quilting

↳ Sports Equipment; Parachutes

↳ Fabric Sculpture

↳ Monogramming & Custom Embroidery

↳ Planes, Boats & Automobiles

↳ Horse Industry, Luggage

Chapter 13

Handmade Specialty Items: Wearables, Heirloom Sewing, Church Linens

Do your friends and family benefit at holidays and other special occasions from your urge to create lovely gift items? When you venture into gift shops do ideas of beautiful things you could make pop into your head? Turn your needleart hobby into a business. An artistic "bent" that took an acute angle provided the success for those profiled in this chapter.

Though he takes issue with the term "wearable art", **Kenneth King** has made his fine reputation with nearly museum-quality vests, hats and jewelry. (According to King, "the term 'wearable art' sounds like art to embarrass yourself in"). Kenneth's story begins in 1984, when he became dissatisfied with his job in Macy's display department... and the two hours of commute it entailed. Kenneth says, "I asked myself: if money were no object, what would I do?" He quit his job. He then took a job in a far less prestigious store (a real motivation to succeeding in his own business), much closer to his home. Each day after work, he would rush home, "as if I had a second job", and work at his fledgling business. "I made it a point to do something towards the success of my business every day; I was committed to it", he says.

For two years, Kenneth worked towards his goal. With the belief that hats would be important in the coming years, and provide a way to make a name for himself, he designed a line of hats and tried to market them for an average of $400 apiece. With little success, and the feeling that he was "throwing money down a big black hole,"

King invited an acquaintance for a networking lunch. He asked his guest, a well-respected manufacturer of knitwear, for her suggestions on how to light a fire under his business. She asked him how much he was selling the hats for, and when Kenneth told her, she promptly replied "Double the price." She explained that his work was unique, and his target market could and expected to pay more for outstanding creative efforts. He should go after their business aggressively.

That was in the summer of 1986. In the following months, his jewelry teacher's sister, a photo stylist, agreed to act as his agent and help market some of his pieces. On the Tuesday before Thanksgiving, as Kenneth sat at his kitchen table pondering whether to use his last few dollars "to pay the phone bill, or to buy something to eat for Thanksgiving", the phone rang. It was his agent: she had placed some of his beaded and embellished, adjustable-fit halter vests at Maxfield, the prestigious Los Angeles store. The next morning, performer Cloris Leachman bought the first one, at $2,100. The store knew a good thing when they saw one, and they launched Kenneth King's success in grand style. Since then, King has designed a new vest each year. Many of Maxfield's customers collect them; the average buyer, according to King, owns six.

In 1987, Kenneth quit his job and rented a studio in San Francisco. The October stock market crash made many of his retail accounts nervous, and they began reducing orders on his more pricey items. This sudden unfortunate turn in economics forced King to give up his apartment and move into his studio. In order to reverse "putting all my eggs in one basket", he began creating "marble" jewelry – sterling silver pieces incorporating marbles, that his customers could wear "during the day". He also began teaching at the Sewing Workshop. "Income from more than one source was very appealing, at this point".

Meanwhile, King's hat sales were gathering steam, attracting many movie star clients, including Geena Davis and Don Johnson. Buyers received the beautifully made hats in a hand-crafted (by Kenneth) velvet hatbox. The box alone is a work of art. Kenneth says he knew he had made it when Elton John wore one of his $3,000 creations when he starred in a Diet Coke commercial. Though some of his work is heavily embellished, King says "My work has to live in the world and be comfortable to wear. I want it to go to parties, and attend chic affairs, and go to Europe. I want my customer to enjoy the things I put my label on."

Heirloom Sewing

AnnMarie Wilson had trouble finding an heirloom quality christening gown for a cousin's baby, so she decided to make one. The results of her first one were so pleasing, AnnMarie went on to make four more for friends. Her husband suggested turning her avid interest into a business, and even suggested a name for it: "Blessed Events". From the start, he has encouraged her home business. "He realizes this isn't a game; this isn't a pastime," says Wilson. It's a good thing he has such a realistic attitude, because she says "I eat, breathe and sleep sewing." She is so deeply involved in the fine sewing arts that she was a contributing editor to the Sewing & Fine Needlework Guild's quarterly magazine. She was also the Chairperson of the Masters Fancy Work by Machine Committee for the now defunct Sewing & Fine Needlework Guild.

Wilson makes European-style christening gowns, 42-45 inches long, sometimes made of poly/cotton batiste, but often made from fine cotton or even silk batiste, in "true Victorian style". Wilson experiments all the time, and has successfully duplicated some older techniques with modern materials. It took a laborious three months for AnnMarie to turn one hundred and sixty yards of tea dyed strip lace into a gown. Wilson realized that she could never sell the dress for enough to compensate for her labor, so it has become a display piece at a shop where she sells much of her collection. The piece acts as a conversation starter, and has brought Wilson much of her business.

Wearables

Current strong interest in art-to-wear and the hand-crafted look also keeps AnnMarie busy creating jackets and vests. In addition, she says "Wearables brought color back into my life. The christening gowns are lovely to work with, but after awhile, all those soft tones get boring". Wilson likes to do plenty of hand beadwork on these jackets, which also often boast cutwork designs, many reflecting the wild Texas look people in her area love. The shapes of armadillos, chilies, and cactus is not what one usually thinks of when imagining a cutwork vest, but that's a design Wilson has copyrighted. Add a splash of metallic thread running through the design, reminiscent of barbed wire, and the Western theme is complete. She usually wears her new design experiments, in part, to generate excitement in customers. One recent addition to AnnMarie's line is a five-layer "broomstick" style skirt, which is a popular Western look. It looked like a challenge to make for sale profitably, because "every minute counts when the clock is ticking". Wilson found a way to gather all the layers in one pass on her serger using a special foot.

Because of arthritic hands, Wilson likes to alternate products. "Living in a warm climate helps, too", says the Garland, Texas resident of the arthritis. Also, switching tasks keeps her interested in projects. "It re-energizes me to have a change. I can go back to what I was doing before and see it with a fresh eye." Teaching gives her yet another break from sewing, and the store where she sells her christening gowns holds her classes on their premises.

Sandy Mooney is another fiber artist . With a mom who was a teacher in a one-room schoolhouse, growing up "you always made stuff". The coats and jackets that are her specialty are quilted, dyed, painted, beaded and otherwise embellished into a one-of-a-kind end product. The "bloomin' vest technique" Mooney uses in her quilting was developed in Renaissance times for hunting coats. The roughed texture of the cloth blended in better with its surroundings, and provided more warmth. Of course, the artistic, beaded creations Mooney produces bear no resemblance to hunting coats!

Mooney credits Design Works with inspiring her creativity. Design Works is a Flushing, Michigan group of nearly two dozen women artists. Members, primarily weavers, meet monthly, and take turns assigning a new project for the others to explore. Sandy says she has learned a lot from these projects, and has tried things she never would have attempted on her own. The support of the others and their help on techniques makes experimentation more practical. Since each person is doing the same project, if she has difficulty she usually finds she isn't the only one, which helps her confidence level. Learning new things also fits right in with Sandy's business philosophy. As she says: "Creativity is a never-ending process; one thing leads to another."

Sandy sells most of her inventory at art fairs and craft shows. When her husband was on strike at General Motors and had no benefits, Mooney began stockpiling projects for sale at shows, starting with batiks and lace teddy bears. Back in the early 60's when the shows were free, she organized her own booths. "Now the entry fees can be as much as $500," she says. Most of the people selling at the shows are in their early fifties, like Mooney, and regard their involvement as a business. "It wasn't taken seriously back when I started; then it was a hobby kind of thing. Now it's a business." Until recently, Mooney says, it was hard to get insurance or a loan from a bank. Sandy feels it's significant that both institutions now recognize art and craft industries more readily.

Pricing the Work

Pricing, that old bugaboo, was hard for Sandy at first. Once she began thinking of what she does as a "service", it seemed automatically worth more to others. "When people put a dollar amount on their time, they get paid for it. It's all in how you perceive yourself," she says. Though she feels that money shouldn't be a measure of your worth, it often is anyway. When friends or neighbors ask her to make something for them, she replies, "'I'll be glad to make X for you, if you'll come over and do my ironing, laundry and my other chores for me.' This usually turns them right off. It's hard for women to learn not to waste their time, and that all time has value. " It's a hard lesson to learn in the beginning, and some never figure this out, but if a profit is to be made, it's important to keep this idea forefront in your mind.

Art and Craft Fairs

Sandy calls the art fair life "camping out in your good clothes". She describes visiting the Porta-john in nylons, and living, gypsy-like, for three to four days in tents. One street fair in Ann Arbor was unforgettable. There were tornado warnings, and it began raining. Police came running, yelling for everyone to "get off the street". A furious wind kept Sandy from doing little more than tucking her small son in among the pillows and batik things, and riding out the storm. At the end, everybody was okay, but her charge slips, which had been in a wicker basket, were "in a soggy ball".

Now, automatic strip readers for charges are available, which can be hooked up to a cellular phone. This wonderful convenience has made the art fair way of life much safer, too. "I can call for emergency help if I need it", says Mooney. "And I can call out for a pizza, if I get hungry." Overnight at the motel room, Mooney recharges the cell phone. She says slogging through mud and lugging heavy boxes is a crazy way to make a living, but she still enjoys it. (For more on craft shows, see the next chapter.)

Church Linens

While you probably won't get wealthy beyond belief sewing church linens, it can be a satisfying and fulfilling addition to your business. There are several books that can help you get started in this specialty, but knowing your own denomination's requirements for various celebrations will give you a good background. Just be aware that a non-profit corporation is buying your commissions, and that the process often involves going through a church procurement committee.

Commissioned work is special. When taking on an assignment, even with a church, it's often in your best interest to have a written contract. Asking for a deposit is a good idea to help defray expenses and protect the artist from the buyer's caprices about whether to pay. A carefully worded contract can also prevent the artist's work from being reproduced and sold without her permission, and will offer protection for the buyer, as well. Consult with an attorney if you are offered a contract you do not fully understand, or if you wish to have one drawn up. The operative Murphy's law seems to be that if you don't have a contract, you'll wish you had. Sometimes, the person for whom you do the most, and to whom you give the best deal, is the one who doesn't pay. Let the seller beware! In addition to consulting an attorney, there are several fine books written specifically for crafters, with boilerplate legal forms included. (See Bibliography.)

Chapter 14

Craft & Boutique Items

Creating and selling products for the craft show circuit and boutiques can be a way of life, and add to your bank balance, too.

Professional Crafters

Though the demand for hand-crafted goods has increased, raw materials manufacturers and retailers still often give the craft producer a difficult time. To help make a better profit, craft producers need to buy raw materials at wholesale cost. (The more minimal packaging of volume necessities is also desirable – a gallon of paint, for instance, as opposed to many two-ounce bottles, or 30-yard put-ups of ribbons or laces, vs. small packages of lace). Suppliers, both retail and wholesale often feel the craft producer is not a serious businessperson, and/or that they are competing for the same consumers' dollars. Craft producers have a reputation as part-time hobbyists who either give away their output as gifts, make them for themselves, or, if they actually sell the finished goods, sell such a small amount that it doesn't qualify as a business. Traditionally, retail stores have been reluctant to offer discounts to craft producers, and manufacturers have made it difficult for crafters to buy directly. Since an average craft business profit margin is in the 20-30% range, the cost of raw materials can mean the difference between success and failure of the enterprise.

A March 1993 article in *Craft & Needlework Age* magazine, a trade publication for craft store owners, devoted six pages to the tensions between the retail supplier and craft makers. The article offered several suggestions to the retailers for getting the crafter's business without antagonizing her. Retailers were urged to offer sliding scale discounts to the pros, based on their dollar volume of purchases, increasing as the purchases increased.

Manufacturers sometimes present a host of new hurdles for craft producers. They usually require large minimum orders (especially initial orders), proof of ordering from another manufacturer of a minimum dollar amount within a previous time frame, letterheads and payroll checks. Ironically, the craft producer must, for all intents and purposes, "audition" to buy from the source! Some suppliers go as far as asking to see the producer's Schedule C from their most recent personal income tax return.

An alternative to this scrutiny is to join a craftperson buying cooperative. This may or may not work for you. Be sure that others in the co-op are dealing with manufacturers whose products you can use, and that the administration is equitably compensated. Be sure there are provisions made to deal with members who are slow or non-payers. A convenient distribution location might also be important, especially if you order frequently.

In recent years larger chain stores have either bought up the small, independent stores, or merely price warred them out of business. In a sign of a reversal of this direction, merchandise distributors are looking to the independents for more of their business. The March 1993 issue of *PCM Magazine* quoted the president of Sullivan's, US, an Australia-based crafts and pattern supplier, as preferring the small, independent craft retailers. "Small fish are sweet, and we would rather have 4,000 or 5,000 independent accounts buying from us than one big chain with 2,000 or 3,000 stores." The April 1993 issue of the same magazine expressed firm belief that smaller stores will dominate the craft picture in the near term.

What does this mean to craft producers? It should mean that manufacturers will be more amenable to selling raw materials to you for your business, since they are already dealing with many more small accounts than in the past. Also, retailers will gradually come to realize that you are not a threat to their business. One professional crafter says the store where she originally bought her goods and received a fair discount still gets her business when she is testing new products and requires small amounts of products. She also recommends them to home crafters, or those testing the waters for a business. This kind of loyalty is necessary for the smaller stores who rely heavily on repeat business.

While buying at wholesale is usually desirable, it is not always possible, especially if the producer is only using a small amount of product. Manufacturers need to sell large volumes at wholesale prices and often don't want to bother with orders below a certain dollar minimum, often $100 or more. In this case, craft producers can control costs simply by watching for sales at local stores.

Running Your Business

A word of caution: because the retailers and manufacturers feel some hobbyists have abused wholesale buying, professional crafters have come under much scrutiny in the past few years, and not just from suppliers. A recent Internet posting spoke of IRS agents visiting flea markets to check on resale licenses and sales records. Anyone without these proofs of having a legitimate business paid steep penalties.

Another pitfall to avoid is the use of commercial or copyrighted patterns in product manufacturing. This type of intellectual property is more stridently protected by their creators today, a consequence of misuse by part-time and even professional crafters. It's not unheard of for authorities to confiscate stock in such a situation. Exercise care to use only original designs in your products.

Trade Shows

Another positive direction began in California in 1988, with the opening of the Beckman's Crafts Supplier Show, the first trade show for those who make crafts for resale. The craft producers attending were allowed buying access, as they were pre-qualified upon registration by the show producers. The show required attendees to present two forms of business identification. In 1992, another show began, the Professional Crafters Trade Show, by Offinger Management in Columbus, Ohio. In 1993, three different cities hosted this show. Handicraft manufacturers, according to a May 1993 article in *PCM Magazine*, are the second largest category of membership in ACCI (Association of Crafts and Creative Industries). In order to gain admittance to the ACCI shows, professional crafters must submit, in addition to their resale tax certificate, three other proofs of business. Another group, HIA (Hobby Industries of America), has similar requirements.

Sales Tax

A frequent area of confusion for many craft producers is the handling of sales tax. Just because a business has a resale number it doesn't exempt them from paying sales tax on everything they buy. Sales taxes need to be paid (except in states that have no sales tax) by the end user of the item, regardless of whether they have a vendor's license or a resale number. The tools and equipment used by a business owner are generally taxable, but the materials used in the manufacture of a final product are not. Simply stated, just be sure that someone pays the taxes – usually the customer who buys the finished goods. This misunderstanding gives retailers (who must account for the sales taxes they charge, so they can pay their home state) a major headache, making them reluctant to accept craft producers as regular, discounted customers.

Selling at Shows

Traveling around the country to the many craft shows that abound can be a profitable enterprise, and an exhausting one. The necessity of having all the products with you can be daunting, particularly for long tours, when there are no stops at home in between shows. It can be disastrous to run out of stock in the midst of a show, where you have paid the booth space fees in advance. Good planning is essential, as are stockpiles of product to sell. Also, because the same customers often attend their favorite shows year after year, a craftperson should have a new merchandise mix each time.

Are you interested in attending a juried show? If so, you may have to submit slides of your work for evaluation. Spending the time and money for quality slides of your products will a big difference in getting approval. Poor quality photos won't show your work to best advantage, and gives a bad impression of your standards for quality and professionalism.

Also, target shows based on the customers they might draw. If your product is higher in quality than one normally expects to see at a mall craft show, it might be wise to exhibit at shows which attract patrons with greater balances in their checkbooks.

Mail order crafts

Giselle Blythe has done well as a craft show exhibitor . Specializing in cats, she has turned her lifelong love of the furry creatures into a business that is fun to run. It began when she created a stuffed cat for a favorite nephew. The cat was such a hit she decided to make half a dozen to sell at a state fair in Washington. They sold out in only two hours. This launched her into business, and Giselle spent that entire summer at craft shows and fairs.

At one of the shows, a shop owner approached and asked Giselle to wholesale her critters to him. This was a good situation for Blythe for several years, until the shop closed. A new shop in the same area is carrying her goods now, but Giselle decided she needed to diversify so that she wasn't relying so much on one client.

Branching out to wearables, Giselle designed an embellished T-shirt called "My Cat Walks All Over Me", which she advertised in *Cat Fancy* magazine. It "sold tons", and from these sales, Blythe developed a customer and mailing list. A "Cat"alogue with 10-15 constantly changing items is sent periodically to the 2,500 or so names she currently has on her "A" mailing list (after purging). Advertising and press releases contributed to its success, and further aided by the visibility Blythe has gotten from the many stores around the country that carry her various wearable and decorative items. Handpainted scarves and shirts, cat toys and cat jewelry are included in her current product list, carried by about 50 different accounts.

An article by Barbara Brabec about Blythe and her cat-related business in *Crafts Magazine* opened the door for Giselle to write a regular feature in *Cats Magazine*. Her husband, who is a graphic designer, takes photos of projects, and she writes the instructions for cat crafts for the magazine. More of her patterns are being published, and Giselle sells them at shows along with her other products. Her husband also helps with the publicity for the line, drawing on his experience in this area.

Blythe cites several professional organizations that have contributed to her success. Machine Embroidery of Oregon and Washington, or MEOW, (appropriately enough for Giselle), and the California Machine Embroidery Art (CAME), are excellent sources of information on lace-making, thread painting, decorative threads and quilting techniques. Another tremendous source of data has been the Seattle Textile Computer Users Group (STCUG – see Sources), for which Blythe has served as treasurer. Each month, this group has a meeting exploring a different subject, such as pattern drafting, knitting machines and weaving looms that can be hooked to a computer. Desktop publishing for craft design and publishing craft patterns has helped Blythe more easily submit designs to magazines for publication, broadening her audience.

Raw Materials

Giselle, whenever possible, buys materials wholesale. Silk scarves and T-shirts are purchased in bulk from a couple of different warehouses, as are totebags and aprons (which Blythe's designs embellish). Ziplock bags are bought in large quantities. For the stuffed cats, and their little friends the mice, Giselle buys unpelted longhair fur and rat fur by the bolt directly from the mill or a warehouse. Bolt ends of the same goods are available occasionally, as well.

Small Accessories

Small craft shows are where you'll find Sheila Harrington. A limiting ordinance in Arizona keeps her from going too far afield. In order to sell in each city in the state, Arizona requires a separate yearly license. For local shows, a monthly application must be made. Bridal is her specialty; she likes to make the headpieces, garters, and all the other accessories that make the occasion remarkable for the bride on her special day. Coordinating all of these elements gives Sheila a great deal of satisfaction. She would like to be able to get into the larger, more expensive regional bridal shows in order to expand. However, with the small base of operations she has now, it's been difficult for Harrington to build her business.

One-of-kind Items

Milwaukee wearable artist **Nancie Needles-Chmielewski** handpaints beautiful silk scarves and garments . Starting with scarves was an easy intro to silk-painting for Nancie. Stretching them on a frame, "the design is hand-drawn, using a resist called gutta. I then paint over it and let the colors go where they will!" Often, she paints earrings in the same patterns to make a set, then packaged together, increasing the amount of each sale. Expansion into clothing painted in the yardage state, prior to cutting out and sewing, followed the scarves. Adapting her own patterns, Needles-Chmielewski designs dresses, skirts and other garments. Some of her latest creations include vests and jackets, which are hand-painted, quilted and beaded, sometimes to coordinate with several other silk pieces in her collection. Besides special request items, scarves and earrings, Needlesworks (Nancie's company) sells handpainted all-silk accessories, including scarves, ties and camisoles.

In-Home Marketing

Employing a one-of-a-kind marketing strategy, Nancie works a little differently from others in the craft show domain. Nancie infrequently shows at art fairs because she prefers the more comfortable, target marketing approach of in-home shows, where a small group sees her newest line. Making a list of people she thinks might appreciate the unique quality of her garments, Nancie invites them to an informal evening get-together. "I hate to be pressured into anything; this makes it real hard for me to press others to buy," she says. Her low-key approach must work; at her first home show, half of the guests bought from her. According to Nancie, fall is the best time for in-home or office shows, when people are looking for holiday gift ideas. Her mailing list has grown by adding the names of people she meets at the shows, and the referrals that came from those who have bought from her. A seasonal promotion, showing some of her latest items and giving dates of upcoming shows, gets sent to the names on this list she's developed. Because of bad experiences with retailers, she has not been aggressive in getting her stock placed in a retail setting.

As a small business owner, Nancie has to "pace" herself. She doesn't actively sell right after Christmas, or in the summer, choosing instead to build up her inventory of stock during these slack sales times. Preferring the pure design process, and being drawn to the creative side of the business, Nancie has had to develop good business sense. ("It's hard to wear lots of hats," she says.) Hardest was overcoming the desire to give "deals" to people when they want her products. Squelching this impulse is helping her make the business pay. Also, Nancie is working with an image consultant, who designs and coordinates styles for her clients. "A symbiotic relationship" is how Nancie describes the partnership.

Craft Malls

A new wrinkle on the craft scene is the arrival of the craft mall. These stores are appearing all over the country, usually adjacent to busy shopping areas. The crafter rents space in the "mall", which is a permanent booth space, similar to those in traveling mall shows. A monthly fee allows the crafter to place his or her goods in the booth, arranged whatever way they wish to display them (within certain guidelines). When the products are sold, the craft mall takes in the money, maintains the major credit card accounts, and pays the crafter at regular intervals. There is a security system in most of the stores, and the crafter doesn't ever have to be there. Be aware, this could be a drawback if your product is one you need to demonstrate to sell it effectively. Sharing space is an option, for those just starting out; you need less merchandise, with less risk to each exhibitor.

Consignment Shops

Other ways to sell art and craft wares without actually being present include selling on consignment to gift shops, quilt or fabric stores. If the product mix is right for the store, the crafter may profit nicely. Sometimes, restaurants, banks, libraries and office buildings display art with ordering or purchasing information. A professional-looking portfolio of other items should be available for those times when a multiple sale is a possibility. Sandy Mooney recommends that those interested in selling crafts or art items subscribe to *The Crafts Report,* which is a good resource and offers networking opportunities. Another publication is the *National Home Business Report* which she also regards highly. (See Resources.)

Chapter 15

Banners, Flags, Kites & Windsocks, Church Banners

Ever since Betsy Ross made her prototype, there has been a good market for American flags. Elizabeth Ross (and her daughters and granddaughters), continued to make flags for over fifty years.

But there is more to the flagmaking story than the Star Spangled Banner. Many cities have banners flying in their downtown areas. Schools and businesses use banners for identity and a variety of other reasons. Museums, trade shows and horse owners require banners for vastly different purposes. Boat owners often request flags, as do schools. One of the latest suburban trends is the flying of seasonal banners in front of private homes.

Commercial Banners

Reneé Morgenstern, a textiles major in college, began her banner-making career at the Ohio Historical Society as a volunteer. Her work there attracted the attention of the group putting together exhibits for the then-new Kentucky Horse Park. The company that designed the Horse Park asked Reneé to submit a bid for manufacturing banners to their specifications to decorate the horse farm history museum.

Morgenstern had five months to research and prepare for the bid. As much out of inexperience as anything else, she was the low bidder and won the contract. This was the start of a new venture for Reneé – designing and manufacturing banners of all types and sizes. "They put me in business", she says. "Working with topnotch designers was inspiring." They hired her to do other museum projects and to make all the horse-related decorative items of the one-of-a-kind Las Vegas Hilton Sports Book. This is an area of twelve different 12 foot-high video screens where bettors can wager on sports events all across the country. (See Chapter 22 for more on Morgenstern.)

Drum Corps Flags

Just as Reneé Morgenstern found a niche of her own, **Barbara Shelton** also fills a unique need. When I originally heard that Barb made flags, I naturally that she made American flags, or perhaps long plain banners with silk-screened designs on them. In short, the wrong thing.

Then Barbara asked me to help her with an especially busy flag season. I got a firsthand chance to get straightened out. The flags that Barb makes are pure fantasy. Color guards and drum corps use them in elaborate routines that undulate across a football field with the crisp precision and color of a Chinese New Year's dragon dance. Rather than being appliquéd or silk-screened, the designs fit together like a huge jigsaw puzzle.

Modern day drum corps routines date back about 50 years ago, to when a Madison, Wisconsin Boy Scout troop offered a Drum Corps merit badge. This soon spurred creation of other drum corps, now found all over the world. They compete with one another with gusto. The Madison Scouts Corps is still in existence today and remains one of the top ten in the world, according to Shelton.

Members, 13-21 years old, must be proficient in percussion or horn instruments, or in the "color guard" – the choreographed group which carries and manipulates the colorful flags like those Barb makes. In one year's competition, the Madison group performed to Gershwin's "Rhapsody in Blue", marching along a 30 yard long silk-screened piano keyboard. The color guard "spun" 30 piano keyboard flags in time to the music, flags that had piano keys screened to them by Banners by Barbara.

These flags are truly creative efforts, usually designed jointly by Barb and the guard director. The director will often bring a sketch of an idea inspired by the choice of music, and some color combinations. Barb then adds her own ideas, some inspired by her more than 600 original designs, hung from the rafters in her workroom. In addition, Shelton often suggests changes to the design that make the flags "spin" or "fly" better. They must be aerodynamically sound in order to work properly on the field.

Lest you think this is just a matter of sewing and creative design, Barb hastens to add that a thorough knowledge of the musical piece is necessary to accurately interpret the mood needed by the guard. Some shows require the use of as many as four separate sets of flags. Barb also adds other little touches that no other manufacturer has: proper finishing so that the much-used fragile fabrics do not fray, and a special corner fold so the edge doesn't whip into the person using the flag.

Barb's career began when her daughter Pam was in band in seventh grade. Since she enjoyed sewing, Barb began doing favors – fixing uniforms, etc. Then Pam went to the guard as a freshman in high school. The band director's spouse asked the kids if they knew anyone who could sew their flags that year. Pam, a proud daughter, naturally volunteered her mom!

It didn't take long for other schools to notice the superior quality of Barb's work and how well her custom designs flew. Schools from all over began to order flags and her fame spread across the country. At any given invitational meet, Shelton can claim a number of the participants as her customers. A batch of her guard flags was once taken to England for a performance for the Royal Family. Her flags have also flown in several Macy's parades.

The materials used in flags range from ripstop nylons, to tissue lamés, to silks. One particularly drop-dead gorgeous flag made of velvet lamé used in combination with black net, which disappears at a distance, fairly shimmered in the sun. The result was stunning.

Shelton's business is seasonal and very different from, say, a dressmaker's. In the busy season, from June through September, she often works 18-hour days. She has made as many as 4,000 flags in a single summer.

Patternmaking

Ralph Shelton is an important part of Banners by Barbara. An accountant who also works at home (he works upstairs, she's taken over the entire basement), Ralph several years ago discovered that his expertise in math made him a whiz at patternmaking for the intricate designs of the flags. He uses pattern paper and a calculator to refine designs to make them more aerodynamically accurate. He also makes sure the many pieces of some of the very intricate patterns fit together well.

Banners by Barbara come in a wonderful array of shapes, sizes and colors. Barb says she once had an order for a banner that measured 80 feet square. In order to fold it up for shipping, they went to the nearest parking lot. When it was too windy there, a high school gymnasium proved to be the answer.

Outdoor Flags

The recent trend towards decorative outdoor flags has given **Karen Bunnell** of Concord, North Carolina a home-based design, mail order and manufacturing business. When a friend asked her to make "one of those Halloween flags", Bunnell whipped one up, using a commercial pattern. She so enjoyed it that soon she was making and selling her own designs. Her skill at appliqué came in handy for the multicolored depictions of various holiday and seasonal subjects.

Karen's Krafts came into being in March of 1992, and represents Bunnell's first effort at sewing for profit. Bob Bunnell does the paperwork and sends out brochures for the mail order portion of the business. This enables Karen to concentrate on designing and sewing the colorful custom flags.

An important facet of Karen's Krafts is Bunnell's color catalogue of original flag patterns. Twelve pages of about 70 designs for those who choose to make their own, sell for about $3.50 each. In addition she sells flag fabric by the yard. The custom flags Bunnell herself makes usually run $60-70 apiece for a 34-by-50 inch flag, less for the smaller, "garden" sizes.

Church Banners

As a service to her church, **Karen Watson** of PHD Sewing Studio in Virginia began making liturgical banners. "This is a good outlet for my creative energy," she says. "There's lots of design work; the designs must be submitted to a committee at the church and approved." Her specialty is 10 foot long banners, appliquéd and sewn. Through experience, she has refined their design. "Ten feet of fabric lies fine and flat on a table; hung up, it billows and does other things you wouldn't expect." Her techniques now produce banners that behave as planned.

For one church's capital campaign dinner, Watson enlarged the church's logo and applied it to a banner. Logo banners are popular, and are especially helpful as identification for the churches when they have regional conferences and interchurch activities. One of Karen's most challenging projects was a four-part Advent banner. It was Velcroed together, piece by piece, over the four weeks. On the last Sunday, removal of the last piece revealed the word "Peace" down one side. In the interim weeks, the letters formed a different design.

PHD's success in relies to a great extent on Karen's knowledge of the liturgical symbols. If you are planning to break into this market, familiarize yourself with the symbols and designs used in various ceremonies by different religions.

How to Succeed

If flag and banner making seems appealing, be sure to find plenty of space for cutting and measuring. You will also need industrial sewing machines to handle the heavier fabrics often used, and to speed up the actual sewing process, which can be tedious with its long stretches of seams.

Access to a computerized lettering system can also be helpful, according to Shelton. Banners often display the name of a company or institution, so quality lettering is important for the customers. A computer program helps ensure all the letters are proportionately sized. Shelton contracts for letters through another producer who specializes in commercial banners.

An ability to draw or execute logos or designs to scale is important, too. Most schools and businesses have an easily recognizable graphic insignia, without which all banners would look alike. This logo often incorporates all or a portion of the name of the client. A helpful tool for this is an overhead projector.

Other opportunities of this kind include making kites and windsocks. Because these are generally made of colorful, lightweight fabrics, a domestic machine can be used to get started. Craft shows, retail specialty stores, and mail order are all good outlets for sales and marketing.

Chapter 16

Dolls & Doll Clothes, Puppets & Toys

Parlay your knowledge of period dolls, or other "toys" or collectible items into a successful career devoted to designing and making purely pleasurable products. Doll collecting has become a leading hobby, right after stamp collecting in popularity. And no self-respecting doll can remain naked!

Doll Clothes

Lynn Noonan got involved in making doll clothes when she made some outfits for her daughter's Cabbage Patch doll. A neighbor saw them and urged Noonan to make some to sell. Lynn used some fabric she had on hand and whipped up a batch for a show outside Toledo, in Perrysburg, Ohio. Everything sold. This experience was repeated at another show. Soon, she was buying fabric especially for doll clothes, in tiny prints, such as the knits used in Health-Tex and Oshkosh children's clothing. Keeping her eyes open while shopping has paid off; she's found fabric from these companies, and on occasion, from Baby Dior on the flatfold table at Hancock's. Sometimes the material is flawed, but according to Lynn, this is easy to work around with doll clothes,. Watching closely for sale items helps her keep her prices uniform.

Noonan says she can make $4,000-5,000 in a single weekend. This represents a lot of doll clothes, so a show takes several weeks of sewing work. Her latest leading styles are for the American Girls Collection, sold by the Pleasant Company of Middleton, Wisconsin. Each of the five dolls, based on a different period of American history, has her own wardrobe. The clothing sold in the catalogue, which is quite pricey, is all historically accurate. Because the company puts out books about each doll, the fans of these characters want their doll's clothing to be similar to that portrayed in the books. Noonan approximates each look, in a somewhat simpler way, which lowers the cost of the tiny garments. She began testing the market for this branch of her work in 1991, then "watched it take off". The dolls are $88 apiece, and people expect to pay more for the clothing, so Noonan can charge more for these styles, increasing her margin nicely.

Whenever she makes a sale Noonan asks the customer if they would like to be on her mailing list. In this way, she has built a carefully screened list for her twice a year postcard mailing. The computer addressed postcards tell potential customers where she is selling her wares.

These days, Lynn goes only to juried shows, for which there are many limitations. The Toledo Craftsman Guild puts on eight such shows a year, of which Noonan usually participates in four. "They are particular as to what you put on your table," she says. "You must have made everything, and it must be a certain percentage hand-crafted, as opposed to assembling ready-made parts. Products also can't be mass produced, and there's a quality standard." While some of the shows take place in outdoor areas, the ones Noonan chooses to attend are in a mall, where there might be 300 booths like hers. She likes this arrangement, because it's free to those attending, and the mall has ample free parking. She also thinks the sales are better at the free shows. On Thursday, the first day of a show when the mall is not busy, she often sells out of her best merchandise, mainly because of her mailings.

Dressing Dolls

Margaret Marinucci makes doll clothes part time for just one customer. This customer who is a doll crafter who makes dolls that are all fabric, stuffed, and have painted faces. this customer/boss participates in juried doll shows, and sells to many "nice, Bucks County touristy shops." In 1992, the doll crafter made over 4,000 dolls, for which Marinucci made all of the dresses. Someone else sews the pantaloons and the doll bodies.

The doll clothes Margaret sews have her name in them, which is great exposure for her other sewn crafts. "In our neck of the woods, crafts are very lucrative, and there aren't many sewn products," she says. The best part is she can keep busy, filling in around her more seasonal children's clothing production with doll work. Juggling this product mix works to her advantage, though she says she makes less on the doll clothes.

Historical accuracy is important with some dolls, especially those traded, collected and sold and depict particular, and sometimes, familiar figures. Costuming these dolls has become a big business since many of the collectors cannot sew, or would simply rather buy the clothing already made. If you find yourself drawn to this type of sewing business, check with doll collectors in your area. Serious collectors will know of the various associations and shows going on. Contacts from such groups may be your best source of business.

Puppets

Polly Trant (profiled in Chapter 8) has made a sideline to her costume business by designing and creating puppets. Though similar in construction to her synthetic fur-costumed mascots, the puppets are much simpler to make. During the summer of 1993, Trant made 2,100 "Dusty Dillo" and "Charlie Roadrunner" puppets. Used for school bus safety education classes in all the Texas schools, Dusty and Charlie are armadillo and roadrunner spokespuppets created in Trant's fertile imagination. Though Charlie is a kind of nondescript bird (maybe even like a duck), old Dusty is quite the fashion plate, with a ten gallon sheriff's hat with a star (and holes for his long armadillo ears), a spiffy vest, buckled belt, and red bandanna. He even sports fancy, fringed Texan gloves. With just bare feathers showing, Charlie can't help being envious.

Chapter 17

Hand & Machine Quilting, Quilt-binding & Ruffling Services

The unique American craft of quilting seems timeless. Once an essential part of pioneer life, quilting remains popular even today. However, the romance of creating lovely patterns, and the satisfaction of joining colors in meaningful ways, Is sometimes stymied by the drudgery of the actual quilting process. As a result, countless beautiful quilts languish unfinished in drawers and quilt presses.

Hand Quilting

From this sad state of affairs, **Ellen Koehn** has pieced together a quilt-finishing business that graces the world with traditional beauty, and provides her pleasurable profit. Ellen started quilting as a hobby, but found that while she liked the hand quilting process, piecing the tops together was not her thing. A friend of hers had a business doing machine quilting, and it appeared to be thriving. So, when Ellen faced a downsizing layoff from her full time job with Weyerhauser, she decided to offer a hand quilting service to augment her income, and hopefully, to segue into a different field.

She put an ad in the company's house newsletter, which went to 5,000 people. An amazing seven jobs came of it, including quilting an old top for a wedding present, which was a very satisfying project for Ellen. After about a year, Ellen did indeed lose her job. She used her payoff package to start her quilting business. This was a big step for her, but the strong response she'd gotten from the advertising in the corporate newspaper gave her courage.

With photos of some of the quilts she had worked on in that year, and some of her business cards (500, the smallest order of cards she could get), Koehn went to a local quilting shop, "very timidly". The shop owner asked to see some samples, and when Ellen tentatively offered that she had some out in the car, the owner gently asked her "Would you like to bring them in?"

This supportive and helpful way of dealing with each other is one of the best parts of doing business with creative business people, and networking with them, says Koehn. "It's so rewarding; entrepreneurs are very supportive. It's a different feeling from the corporate world." In addition, her friends at the quilting shop order things for her immediately and help her whenever they can. Her background in customer service makes her doubly appreciate this help.

"Have a plan, and be willing to change it" is the advice Koehn gives to anyone with a business. For instance, though her focus was on traditional hand stitching, Ellen was looking for ways to speed up her work. She decided to order a Nolting quilting machine for basting. Pushing a queen-sized quilt through her Bernina home machine had given her sore shoulders. The Nolting machine moves easily, and also makes nice patterns. It comes with a choice of table length, the 12' size chosen by Koehn is ample for her needs and she expects it to solve more than one problem.

"Quilting is extremely varied, and there's lots to put into it. If it isn't fun, it's a grind, so you need to keep a fresh outlook," says Koehn. She's fallen in love with beads, and wants to incorporate them in some quilts. "You have to check out what's around you," and knowing that the trend towards art quilts is building, Ellen would like to be regarded as a "quilt artist". While working on other's quilts, many creative ideas have come to her, and she is anxious to implement them in her own designs.

"Putting this out in the universe was an act of faith," Koehn says. "From working in the corporate world, I have the feeling that anything I do that's easy isn't worth anything if it isn't mainline corporate. I also ask myself 'Who do I think I'm kidding?'." Her self-deprecating attitude is the hardest thing to overcome. "I'm just a kid out here; I don't know what I'm doing" is her prevailing self-doubt message. Starting her new business at age 49 may have something to do with this. In her work in the corporation, "everything was structured; there was a book telling you how to do everything, actually, it was often overstructured." While she's confident of the quality of her work, Koehn has a hard time presenting herself and her products. "I watch a daughter who believes in just going for it, and I think it's wonderful she can do her thing without self-doubt."

Part of the impetus behind Koehn's vision for her business was the people with whom she had taken quilting classes. Many of them had made a quilt top and thought they would have a completed quilt at the end of the class. She understood they wanted something to show for the money they spent on the class and materials, but the hand quilting process is too tedious for some people. Her business fills the gap between dream and reality for these erstwhile but often talented quilters.

Some would-be quilters piece for recreation and soon have lots of tops and no quilts. One client had over 300 blocks she had pieced in five years. She asked Ellen to put them together; she didn't care how. Koehn picked out the blocks for quilting, and so far, has made five quilts of them, and has enough blocks left over to make at least three more. She did the construction, the quilting and the binding. "It was wonderful to see these things come to completion", Ellen says. "The look on my customer's face was priceless."

Machine Quilting

While quilts are more valuable if they have been hand quilted, some prefer the look and less expensive service of machine quilting. According to one source, when the sewing machine came into general use, machine stitching was used in even some of the older quilts. **Jenell Noeth** offers her customers machine quilting in addition to machine piecing. Having done dressmaking, Jenell found she could make more money machine quilting in her home in Basehor, Kansas, population 1,500.

In 1983, Noeth took a "quilt as you go" class, building on a lifelong interest, then really got excited about the craft when she discovered the rotary cutter. This little invention made strip piecing easier and faster. At first she paid someone else to quilt her projects for her, but Jenell soon found that she wanted to get a quilting machine. Her new service soon took over the rest of her home-based business.

Between advertising in a local paper and word of mouth, Noeth quickly built a steady clientele. She now sells fabric from her home, although she cannot advertise this fact because of zoning. Extra-wide muslin, 90" and 108" wide, is especially popular for the backings of the quilts that Jenell works on, though some customers provide their own backs. What to charge for her work is a problem, though. Like Ellen Koehn, Noeth feels that since the service seems so easy to her, it must not be worth much, and sometimes she has a difficult time justifying her prices to herself.

A queen-sized quilt can be pinned in the frame and quilted by machine in three to four hours. Templates for Noeth's machine include rose, ivy leaves and raindrops, which she can translate into allover designs. Outline quilting can also be done simply by guiding the arm of the machine around the design in the quilt, outlining 1/8" to 3/8" outside the form. Though many of her clients have pieced their own quilts, Noeth also does outline quilting on printed fabric for a decorator, and is often asked to perform her service for a nearby manufacturer. Noeth was also asked to make a complete set of placemats for the local country club.

Quilt bindings

For speed in quilt bindings, Jenell Noeth bought a Juki commercial machine from a used machine store in nearby Kansas City. Though she bought a binder attachment with the machine, she didn't like the results and preferred instead to sew the binding onto the top, then whip the wrong side down by hand. While Noeth often does binding for her customers, even she cannot do everything. Another person occasionally binds for her, creating another niche in this satisfying specialty.

Other Services

An adjunct to the quilting service is ruffling. Many quilts and bedspreads are trimmed in virtually miles of ruffles, which opens up a whole new business opportunity. Nearly essential to this service is a commercial ruffling machine. An investment in such a machine might be especially beneficial if you work with a decorator or drapery workroom.

Chapter 18

Sports Equipment; Parachutes

Sports Equipment

So many of today's popular sports require specially sewn equipment: rock climbing, cycling, backpacking, golfing, skiing, and skateboarding. A recent trip to Yosemite revealed some of the panoply of gear used by just one of these sports. Sudden winds and rain forced rock climbers, clinging midway up the side of El Capitan, forced to pull special mountain tents around them while they stayed put to weather the storm. Stuff bags and belt carriers held their climbing paraphernalia, and essentials like food and water.

Nearly every sport, including walking around the local mall, requires special packs of some kind. Look around, and see how such things as skis, golf clubs and camera equipment are transported. The development of a clever variation of a product can be the beginning of a company. The knee and elbow pads used by skaters and cyclists are one example of this type of invention. Fanny packs, which began their popularity as hands-free accessories for backpackers and campers, have found their way into chic fabrications and onto the a variety of waists.

Parachutes

In the mid-50's, the sport of skydiving began, with the participants using modified military surplus equipment. The popularity of skydiving rose significantly when the first Vietnam vets came home from their tours of duty. More than any other armed force in history, they had discovered the thrill of jumping out of planes. Some of them loved it, leading them to seek more opportunities for the adrenaline rush it brought.

John Higgins was a jump devotee who saw the potential for marketing better equipment to other fans of the sport. Beginning by offering mail order parts, John soon began designing and manufacturing custom parachutes.

Though the majority of Higgins' business is the sport market, his company does a fair amount of government work, both directly, and as a subcontractor for other companies acting as direct contractors. This kind of work offers its own difficulties. Military contract work requires strictly monitored quality control, and, because of relatively small tolerances, special handling. "The designer (for the military) might have an engineering background, working in something like metals, which require a 1/16" or a 1/8" tolerance. These tolerances are difficult to hold to with our business, though. Fabric, webbing and tapes expand and contract, depending on the humidity. They can literally change size overnight," says Higgins. To deal with this, "You may have to control the days you cut; on days of extremely high humidity, we may not cut at all." This is especially important for his North American Aerodynamics company: their 50,000 square foot factory in sometimes steamy North Carolina is not air conditioned. Regarding the sport market, Higgins says, "The market changes all the time; staying up with it is crucial."

Skydivers can't just go to their local sporting goods store to buy a parachute. A customer relationship normally comes from one of three sources; the skydiving company where they jump, direct from the manufacturer, or from a couple of companies that sell parachute equipment for the manufacturers. Because it's such a specialized activity, most chutes are custom-made for each diver. Prospective clients fill out an order form specifying their color and style choices, which then goes to the manufacturer. A harness container is usually part of the order, and that too is customized. All of these are sewn, not fused, by the 75 to 125 employees of Higgins' company.

Though parachutes were originally made of silk, when nylon was invented, the much costlier silk was no longer used. Silk's air permeability rating is 80 to 120 cubic feet per minute, versus nylons' rating of 0 to 5 CFM. It's easy to see how nylon allows a skydiver or cargo to descend much more slowly to earth. An important safety criteria.

The round, flat canopy style of parachute, like the "GI Joe" image most people have, is still in use, and is considered a true parachute. Newer para-foil styles are the ones most generally used in sport, and nearly always used in world class accuracy competitions, where the jumpers try to land in "targets". The ramair chute is square in shape, with an air foil, or fabric wing, which is steerable, like the wing of a plane, unlike the round chutes. In competitions, "Over 90% of the competitors will be using our products," says Higgins, "We pretty much have no competition; our chutes are proven to be the best." These are all of the para-foil variety of chute. Another type, not made by John's company, is the slope-soaring parachute. This is designed to stay up as long as possible, somewhat like a glider. If the diver, using a slope-soarer, gets into a thermal, there is lift and the chute rises, unlike other types, which lift very little in the same situation.

Anything US military jump personnel or cargo might use is made by North American Aerodynamics. They designed the UM-1 chute especially for the military. Other items they sell include aircraft seat covers for the C-130 troop transport planes, and all the harness fittings. A few years ago, they made an order of 64' cargo parachutes for the Army, like those used to drop supplies by air to the Bosnian refugees in 1993. The tiniest chutes they make are ground signal flare parachutes, which can fit in a back pocket.

How to Decide

If you're a sports devotee and you've invented something that makes your activity more convenient, check the market first to be sure it isn't already on the market. It's amazing how many ideas spring up in more than one place at the same time. If you have a winner, though, you might find a specialty catalogue interested in selling your product. While it is not within the scope of this book to discuss this issue, bear in mind that a high volume of goods may be needed if your product gets a good response. Be prepared to buy all your materials wholesale, in large volume, and be sure your equipment is up to the task. Industrial methods are a must for large scale production. (See Chapter 26.)

Resources

If you're interested in executing your own or someone else's designs in tents, awnings, sports gear, or another heavy-duty product, an industry group can help you find the special fabrics you need. The Industrial Fabrics Association International connects manufacturers with fabric companies. They also publish a variety of publications, including a monthly magazine, *Industrial Fabric Products Review*, *Fabrics & Architecture*, *Safety & Protective Fabrics*, *Data Textile Newsletter*, and other periodicals, as well as many directories, standards manuals, and technical reports. They also publish books on many subjects, from truck covers to awnings, to marine applications. A textile-related information hotline for members is another benefit.

Chapter 19

Fabric Sculpture & Other Fabric Arts

Soft sculpture is a relatively new arrival on the fine art scene, but has become an important one. Fabric can express ideas and emotions in an entirely different way than other media, and has a tactile message, inviting touch and interaction with the art in unparalleled ways. While much fabric sculpture is considered crafty, some very fine pieces truly fall into a fine art category. Participation in art shows may be more your milieu, if your work falls in the art category.

Soft Sculpture

Small acts lead to incredible opportunities, as **Carol Kimball** of Denver found out. When she made a 3/4 life-sized bas relief fabric sculpture of a female figure throwing clay pots for a craft show booth, she had no way of knowing what it would lead to. The booth sold bread bowls, and Carol had made the sculpture for the artist in exchange for a few bowls. When the bowl artist took the piece home, a woman who was organizing a show at the Lincoln Center in New York City saw it and contacted Carol about exhibiting there. This exposure, including having her piece shown on the Today Show, gave Kimball a running start very early in her career; she had only done one large piece, and a few smaller ones.

At first though, Kimball's work seemed to be more popular with other artists than with the general public. Once she made her work more accessible, it helped her sell more. She began working on some well-made, washable, durable puppets. "I took a lot of trouble with the prototypes; I was willing to work the bugs out," before she took them to a show, she says. Her limited mass production of a whole sequence of puppets, together with a series of soft sculptures, got her business going. Depicted were such disparate characters as habited nuns, friars, and Arab sheiks. Carol says she sells a lot of nuns holding rulers. "This seems to generate an emotional response in a lot of people," she says.

Life-sized "icons" (flat-backed) of various figures were another Kimball specialty. Hers were not made of nylon stockings, like so many others at the time, and Carol had to figure out how to seam each individual piece to get the 3-D look. They're big and lightweight, and are easily moved, but still stand up to rough handling. She didn't expect to sell the larger pieces, and was surprised how well they sold, although she priced them high ($500-800 in the early 1980's).

Carol Kimball also creates life-sized dummies for a ventriloquist, with glass eyes she's specially handblown. The orders for this customer are a challenge, as the figures need to move according to their master's decree. One model, the "Lusty Shark", has big lips, a corset and fishnet hose. Carol made a tiny model using the actual fabrics, but the client still had a problem visualizing what she was doing. She realized that she had a better spatial ability than he did, exactly the skill that helped her create the 3-D designs. Which is probably why she can command $2,200-2,500 per dummy!

Kimball says there are five steps to the creative process:

1. The concept: "Gosh, I think I'll make a life-sized nun!"

2. A working game plan: Start with a welded steel frame, make a bas relief to hang on a wall. Plan each step.

3. The actual game plan: "I thought I'd make it of organza, then I ran across this silk, instead." Changes that reflect what you actually did with the project.

4. Finished Product.

5. What the piece becomes after you're done with it.

According to Carol Kimball, "So many people think this type of project is only about #1 and #4. But once it's out of your hands you have no control over what it becomes!

Chapter 20

Monogramming, Custom Embroidery

One of the most perennial of fads is adding one's initials to articles of clothing, handbags and luggage. Somebody always seems to require this service. In recent years embroidery has also grown to include business applications, due to the widespread use of corporate logos on employee clothing.

What Kind of Machine?

The first step in a monogramming/embroidery business – after determining if there's a market in your area – is choosing a machine. For start-up commercial grade machines, there are three main manufacturers: Melco, Meistergram, and Pantogram each have a distinct niche in this market. If you are fortunate enough to live in an area where there are sales reps for the three largest companies, "test driving" the machines is best.

Base your choice of which to buy on several factors, including initial cost, ease of upgrading, and the friendliness of its computer system. For example, how expensive is it to have designs "digitized", or translated into a template for the machine to use? Can you do this step in the process yourself? Find out as much as you can before you commit to a system: these machines begin at $3,000-4,000, and depending on options, their cost can soar into the stratosphere.

Potential Problems to Avoid

One caution, if you are the owner of one of the new domestic embroidery machines meant for the home sewing market: many of the designs included with the machines are copyrighted, and cannot be sold to others. Check with your dealer before deciding you'll add one of these designs to your product list. Also, be aware that these machines are not meant to hold up under the stress of constant use. In general, the speed and durability of the professional quality machines have greater potential to make your business profitable.

How to Find Customers

Once you've determined what system is right for you, and you've mastered its mechanics, finding customers is important! One couple began embellishing premade sweatshirts and caps to commemorate a local annual event. They sold all their product at a street fair, and took orders when they ran out. Getting the items finished in time for the fair was the hard part; the wife worked alone all day, they worked as a team when he came home from work. All their hard work paid off – they almost paid for the initial cost of the equipment within that first month. Word of mouth continues to bring them business, which they treat as a part-time addition to their regular income.

A Georgia entrepreneur bought one small machine to "dabble with" on the side. She was a full time teacher. When she'd made enough to pay for the first machine, she bought a second, adding more capabilities to her workroom. When she has made enough money to pay for this machine, she will buy a third, and quit her regular job. She feels by that time she'll be ready to support herself with monogramming. One of her unusual specialties is embellishing casket blankets. They are used in her area to cover the deceased in their coffin, with the dearly departed's name embroidered across the satin binding.

Storefront Embroidery Business

Linda Walden of Cincinnati has been in the embroidery business in both the retail and wholesale sectors for about 10 years. She had been making aprons for a local company on a subcontract basis, when they told her they sure could use someone to embroider them. She invested in a $23,000 Melco machine, which proved to be a very good business move.

For several years, Linda worked from her home, and for the most part only took on wholesale jobs. In other words, most of her work was for a manufacturer, who then sold the finished product to the end user, usually a chain of stores or restaurants. She soon realized that one customer wouldn't support the initial cost of the machine, let alone her family, so taking on new business became vital. More wholesale clients came her way, and eventually Linda had more work than she could handle. At one point, she and her husband were keeping three machines going around the clock. They had to take turns sleeping. It worked, though; Linda made more in a month than she had previously made in a full year in her business.

Realizing that working like this wasn't much of a life, Walden moved her business, ProSew, to a storefront and hired employees. Until then, Linda had never advertised her embroidery services. All of her business had come through reputation and referrals. Once she was in the store, retail business began coming her way, along with even more of the lucrative corporate work she'd been doing. Walden again moved to an even larger location, and at last count, had five Melco machines in operation.

Pitfalls

There are hazards in this specialty. Some embroiderers refuse to take on the embellishment of any leather items, for fear of ruining them. This is a potential source of trouble for any embroidery job. From the sheer intensity of the stitch, an improperly set up machine can make holes in the project. (Customers usually don't like this.) You might want to find out how insurance can help protect you from such catastrophes. Call your insurance agent and ask him or her if this type of coverage is available before you offer any services. It's best to plan ahead.

Greekwear Embellishment

Nearly every college and university has sorority and fraternity groups, and "Greek"wear is very popular. **Lynn Kist**, also of Cincinnati, has made this her specialty. She gathers articles once a week from a Greek shop (which sells clothing and other personalized items to sororities and fraternities), and returns them as specified on each job order, appropriately decorated. The symbols and initials are appliquéd using a satin stitch. Lynn recommends opening the stitch slightly to increase operator speed. July is her busiest month, with orders coming in from sororities for as many as 90 sweatshirts. She gives a price break on orders of over 50 pieces of the same item.

Things to Consider

Before you invest in a pro-quality embroidery machine, Kist advises finding out how many of the various types of machines there are in your area. "There's a lot of competition here in town; everybody wants to undercut everybody." She has learned that her Meistergram can't compete against multi-head machines, and is concentrating now on the things it does best. Because of the way the needle and the pantogram move, utilizing a zigzag stitch, "Meistergram is the fastest, and does the nicest writing, with a prettier rounded look." Other machines can't round out their designs; the pantogram, or machine bed, moves, but the needle just goes up and down in place. This makes for nicer picture designs which require more detail work.

Another crucial consideration is whether or not to do your own digitizing. Kist would like to have this capability; it would save substantially on her minimum turnaround time of 48-72 hours, even using a fax machine and next-day delivery. The unavailability of someone to digitize custom designs may force an embroidery business to purchase and learn the equipment, an added cost.

Similar Services

Other embellishment services include chainstitching and Omnistitching. Chainstitch machines are controlled by both a hand beneath the table, moving the work, and a hand above controlling the fabric. It takes a certain amount of talent and agility but is in great demand for adding surface texture to school jackets and other sports-type garments. Omnistitch machines are fairly new to the market; they enable the addition of various ribbons, threads, laces, yarns, and cut fabric or other trims to fabric. (See Sources for more information.)

Chapter 21

Planes, Boats & Automobiles

Boat Covers & Sailmaking

The very heavy duty kind of stitching required of producing or repairing boat covers and sails is not for everyone, but the market is there for those interested in taking advantage of its existence. It is especially helpful to have a background in sailing or boating in this specialty, so you have an awareness of some of the special needs of the client. Nearness to a waterway is essential, of course, since customers are more likely to patronize a business close to where they dock their craft.

Since every boat is slightly different, covers are usually custom-made. As in the upholstery business, the ability to measure accurately is vital, since these covers call for a snug fit in heavy weather to be effective. **Bette Dean** of Ohio was once asked to make a cover for an airboat (the kind with the huge propeller on the back). She said yes, under the condition that the owner never tell anyone where he had it done! It was one of her biggest challenges, according to Bette. The owner not only wanted the boat covered, but he wanted the cover to serve as a duck blind, as well! As an upholsterer, Dean had plenty of experience, but working in her driveway for a week was a new one. Jobs like this need to be priced by the hour, since there is really no way to tell in advance what problems may crop up in the course of the job.

Airplane Interiors

Nearly every airport in the country has a shop where owners can go to have their airplanes refitted. This is especially true near smaller, municipal airports. Buyers of used planes are the most frequent customers; they want a fresh, new look for their plane or jet. New seat covers are sewn and installed, and sometimes new curtains, in the larger airships.

Home Dec – for Boats

Refurbishing boats is another specialty. One sewing pro told of a job she had making new curtains for a yacht – 53 pairs! Because all the fittings in boats are usually color-coordinated, opportunities exist for residents of seaports and resort areas. Many crafts require new cushions periodically, and some of the more sumptuous boats have upholstered furniture, including bed coverings.

Auto-Matic

Cars and planes have more than just transportation in common: the seats eventually wear out. Renewing them also requires heavy duty sewing, often with thick vinyls. Access to various automotive fabrics and foams is very important, too. (See Resources for more info.) One enterprising businessperson found that no one recovered motorcycle seats in her area , so she made this her specialty. With several Harley Davidson clubs in her county, she's found a segment of the market that makes a nice sidelight to her upholstery shop.

Car enthusiasts often want special gear to protect their investment. Custom-made covers, protective "bras" for the front of the cars, and distinctive accessories are hot tickets for them. **Marji Ross**, uses her heavy machines to make such unusual items for a company that specializes in offering fancy accessories to MG owners. The owner of the company makes the designs, then he subs the sewing work to people like Ross. Her biggest project for this company is making MG "raincoats". These small sports cars are all convertibles, but when it rains it's not easy to put in the windows, which come out entirely. Ross makes covers that fit over the more easily replaced hood, and incorporate windows in the cover. She says it takes five yards of vinyl for each one.

Furniture Covers

Ross also makes outdoor furniture covers. The company sends her the cut pieces, and she sews them together; she doesn't even turn them right side out afterwards. Marji likes this kind of work, as she can sew piece after piece, chaining them together and cutting them apart later.

Commercial Machine Covers

Who would dream that dog food could offer an opportunity to make money by sewing? **Kelly Harlow** of Kentucky never did, but she has been making the heavy vinyl covers for the screening machines for several years now, and has become a believer. Harlow's dad invented a machine that sorts not only dog food, but tobacco and other products, into desirable-sized chunks. Various sizes of screening keep incdible or unusable pieces out of the product containers. Kelly's vinyl covers fit snugly over the feed tubes, keeping the product from spilling out onto the floor around the machine.

"It's nepotism, pure and simple," says Kelly. She is the only one who makes the covers for the machines her father sells. They come in 10 sizes, from 36" in diameter, up to 83 1/2". Although there are other companies that make covers for similar machines, Kelly says she is the only one whom custom designs covers to fit each individual machine. For instance, one of her customer's, a paint manufacturer, was using a razor blade to cut feed tube holes. Harlow convinced them her custom-made covers would last longer, since the tube sleeves are exactly where they need to be. Lasting longer was desirable: because of the stress created by vibrations of up to 12,000 times a minute, necessitating frequent replacement (as often as 12 times a month). Cutting holes in the cover added to the wear and tear. Kelly's insight into the problem and her solution saved her customer headaches and money, and gave Harlow the job. "Everyone else just told them 'Adjust,' and wouldn't do anything about it." She also often designs covers from detailed drawings and specs provided by the plants.

For nearly all her covers Harlow now uses clear, 12-20 gauge vinyl, which allows the product to be seen as it goes through the screening process. She tried to use muslin for the dog food company's covers, "but they got too greasy, tore, and attracted insects." Many of her clients (like the company that makes tortilla chips) need food grade quality covers, and the vinyl meets specifications. Heavy shock cording (also called bungee cord) holds the bottom edge and feed tube openings snugly, to keep the product from splashing out. Shock cords were initially difficult to attach to the cover. Then Kelly bought a couple of Juki industrial machines which solved the problem – they could finally chew through the vinyl. Periodic time motion studies enable Harlow to price her work well. She also subcontracts some of the sewing work.

Ron Harlow is an important part of Kelly's business; he quit his job a couple of years ago to work full time with her. They have a great division of labor, including the sewing, which Kelly taught Ron. He does much of the finishing work, provides objective quality control, and makes some of the supply runs. "He's learned enough about what I do to know when something's not right. And he's been willing to learn so he can be a vital part of my business." Ron also does all the marketing and keeps the books, for both the vinyl cover business and Harlow's dressmaking business, which she depends on for the variety. "I have a studio full of beautiful fabrics, and a garage full of 20 gauge vinyl," she says.

Chapter 22

Horse Products, Luggage

A serious industry has grown up around the equine world. In the US, horse enthusiasts spend an estimated 3 billion dollars per year on horses and their related needs. Sewn products claim a significant share of this market.

Many Specialties

Equestrian training is a diversified field. Among the disciplines are: polo, thoroughbred racing, English, saddle seat, Western pleasure, quarter horse, dressage, Tennessee Walker, and hunter jumper. Each has different clothing needs for the rider, and many require special horse accessories as well. Casual wear for each discipline is very popular, too.

Hunter jumper trainees begin acquiring horse duds as early as age six. The traditional, everyday uniform includes tan breeches, a tie, and white or blue dress shirt. Tailored suit jackets with gussets for movement, in either navy, "hunter" green, or black, top off the ensemble for everyday wear. "Pinques", which are actually red jackets, are for formal events. Because the costume must fit well for show, the young, growing rider needs to update it often. A tailor who develops a customer base of youthful riders will have business for a long while, as their needs change and grow.

Saddlebred devotees employ more flair in their dress. Their costume tends to be ornamental for both the rider and the horse. Western pleasure riders probably have the most opportunity for sewing creativity. Almost anything goes with this group, who favor fringe, appliqués, fancy chaps, and sometimes, glitz and Lycra. Appealing and original designs are popular with these groups.

A Pattern Business

Linnea Sheppard of Monrovia, California has made a business of supplying patterns to this incredibly diverse industry, with an emphasis on patterns for apparel for saddle seat, English, and hunter jumpers. Sheppard has filled a niche for those who either don't fit in the narrow range of sizes sold by ready-to-wear, or those who want a better fit in riding wear. Her company, SuitAbility, provides a catalogue of styles and specialty notions. A sign of the times, Sheppard's company is also online, at SuitAbil@aol.com, her e-mail address.

While studying for her MBA, Sheppard was in an Entrepreneurial Studies program at Case Western Reserve. As a grad student, she was working with a company that helped start other businesses. Linnea's job was to help prospective business owners fill out forms. She also did market research. While musing at her mother's kitchen table, thinking about different kinds of businesses, she wondered why there were kits like Frostline and Altra for outdoor wear, but nothing for riding clothing. Linnea had nagged her dad to buy her a horse when she was 13, so she had ridden for years. With equal interest, she had sewn for about as long.

Linnea found some books on patternmaking and taught herself to make patterns. She designed some for riding wear, and began selling them as SuitAbility in a newspaper type catalogue. Now she uses a contract patternmaker, but is looking at software programs to evolve her business further. The best program she's found so far would require a $6,000 digitizer.

Sheppard advertises in *Sew News* and all the major horse publications. She feels a circulation of 50,000 is the minimum to make a publication worth her while to advertise.

SuitAbility is primarily a mail order company, but according to Sheppard, the wholesale part of the business grows all the time. "The wholesale business is mostly reactive; I don't seek it out." One Canadian wholesale distributor has exclusive wholesale rights in that country; another distributor in England, a sidesaddle specialist, sells SuitAbility patterns there.

She carries more than 50 patterns, including riding and show apparel, horse blankets, and protective padded items for the horse while it's in a trailer. Her patterns are mostly for saddle seat, English, Western and dressage, though she had so many requests for children's and men's Western clothing, that she wants to branch out. Sheppard gives three reasons why people buy her patterns: "Show apparel really needs to fit well, and they don't make much riding and show apparel larger than size 12 for ladies; the expense of riding apparel; and the desire for unique Western show apparel.

The McCall Pattern Company has a pattern printing service that Sheppard uses. "The Commercial Printing Division at their Manhattan, Kansas plant is wonderful to work with," says Linnea. "They print a minimum run of 1,000 at a time." When customers ask for hardware, she refers them to companies like Rainshed in Oregon. "I'd rather design and sell the patterns." She tries to stay atop trends in show fashions to keep the patterns current. Sheppard rewrites and revises instruction sheets every time they are reprinted, based on customer comments. This is expensive, but Linnea feels it's worth it to keep the quality of her line. She writes the copy for the catalogue, and her sister draws the clever artwork.

In 1993, Breakthrough Press asked Sheppard to write a book about sewing for this specialty. See the Bibliography for more information on *Sew Your Own Riding Clothes*.

Riding Clothes

When her niece began Western and English riding, her trainer asked **Liz Burkhart** to help dress the students. Her first attempt at getting students to turn to her for their habit needs didn't work well; she sent the flyers too late for the April shows. After that, she timed her mailing better, sending her well thought out service summary to most of the stables and academies within a 50-mile radius of her Doylestown, Ohio home. Since then, word-of-mouth has helped her business grow. She also offers custom work through a horse consignment shop. (See more of Burkhart's marketing tips in the Bridal section in Chapter 4.)

Burkhart is pleased with the SuitAbility patterns she uses in this segment of her business. (For more horse-related pattern companies, see Resources.) Offering extensive color choices to her customers has helped make her services very popular with the local students.

One of her most popular items is chaps, which can be made in real suede, or in Ultrasuede, a machine washable lookalike.

Steeplechase

One of the most hidebound and tradition-steeped of all horse pursuits is steeplechase racing. Since the 1600's in England, steeplechase racing has enjoyed a mystique equaled in few sports. The Jockey Club in Great Britain is one of the oldest and most respected sports regulatory bodies in the world. Here in the US the Jockey Club began in Long Island, New York in 1894. Since then, many fine racetracks have continued to provide colorful entertainment in the "sport of kings".

Riders wear the "silks" or "colors" of the owners of their mounts. Each owner has a different color scheme, repeated for the shirts, or silks, of the jockeys, who may change for each race, depending on whose horse they're riding. The Jockey Club regulates the colors and patterns of each New York owner, and keeps files on them to avoid duplication; they used to perform this function for the whole country, but no longer. Today, each state has its own regulatory body for racing, and they keep tabs on the colors used in their state. Solid silks are the oldest; fancier patterns indicate newcomers to the pursuit. In the past, shirts were made of silk, but today they are more likely made of one of three fabrics: lightweight nylon, nylon satin, or aerodynamic 4-way stretch nylon.

In 1978, **Alice Craig** of Lexington, Kentucky began a company called Silks Unlimited, specializing in custom-made racing silks. All of Kentucky, but especially Lexington, is a famous horse breeding area. Lexington is also home to the beautiful and prestigious Keeneland racecourse. Craig sold Silks Unlimited in 1992 to **Patricia Green**, who had been running a thoroughbred horse farm for 20 years.

Green's company is one of the few in the US to make these custom silks, and she says her customers reach the far corners of the world, as well. She claims clients in Germany, France, the British Isles, and the Arab emirates. In addition to silks, Silks Unlimited also makes saddle covers, and tablecloths and pillows with a horse theme. Nearby University of Kentucky and Transylvania University both order flags from Green.

When an owner orders silks from Green, they choose from a variety of swatches and patterns (stripes, checks, diamonds, etc.) on the basic "body", which never varies. Silks Unlimited charges a base price for each fabric; and the more complicated a silk is, the more costly. Since all the jockeys weigh in at around the same weight, about 110 pounds, it is relatively simple to make a silk that fits more than one person. Because owners may have many different jockeys ride their horses, this is convenient. With all the racers' moving around from racecourse to racecourse, the silks often get lost, so replacement orders are common. Green keeps photos of fronts and backs of each design in her files to make replacement orders easier to fill.

Stall Curtains

When the museum banner projects she'd been working on started to thin out (after all, there are only so many museums), **Reneé Morgenstern** had to decide what to do next. (See Chapter 15 for more about banners.) Since she and her family are avid riders, she decided to specialize in this area, particularly making stall curtains for quarter horses. At shows, trainers often decorate their stalls. One order was for thirty stall curtains for the Arab stallions of Las Vegas headliner Wayne Newton. Each curtain took thirty hours to make. Intricate appliqué with the name of the ranch and lots of glitz decorated this luxurious stall decorating project. Four days before the order was due to be shipped lightning hit the Morgenstern home. This didn't stop Reneé, though. She called a sewing friend and together, assembly-line fashion, they churned the work out, right on time.

Horse Accessories

Horse owners also need various hoods, hay and feed bags, saddle covers, tack trunk covers, totes and coolers. Winter blankets are quite a specialty and a necessity to the horse's health. The blankets come in a wide range of styles and qualities. An excellent article in the September 1993 issue of *Horse & Rider* magazine compares the features of several varieties of winter blankets. The prices range from $70 to $236 apiece, and they are anywhere from not weatherproof at all, to 100% water and windproof.

Luggage & Totes

Soft-sided luggage has become a large, diverse field of its own. In the horse industry, for example, carriers for boots, saddles and other gear are very popular. In other sports areas, ski pole and boot totes, and travel bags for golf clubs are in big demand. Camera bags come in a variety of shapes and sizes, too. A fresh approach to organizing the plethora of accessories for either hobbyists or professionals may be just the niche you're looking for. The availability of specialty fabrics like Kevlar or Cordura, and heavy duty zippers and other findings often are vital to good design for such products.

Good marketing, of course, will be a key to your success. Whether you sell to catalogues, independent stores, chains of hobby stores, or by mail order, the possibilities are endless for the right product. One small company mass produces totes for a large mail order firm, which sometimes adds logos, monograms or other embellishments. Fabrics are purchased in bulk, cut and assembled. Several employees using industrial machines sew the individual parts and pass them down to the next station, assembly line style, from the body of the tote, to the strap, to finishing. (For more on production, see Chapter 26. For more on finding specialty fabrics, see Chapter 18.)

PART FOUR:

RELATED FIELDS

↳ Fabric & Notions Sales, Catalogue, Machine Sales

↳ Teaching: Children & Adults

↳ Writing, Video Production, Patterns

↳ Piecework & Factory Sewing

Chapter 23

Fabric Store, Notions Sales: Retail and Catalogue, Sewing Machine Sales

You don't have to have an interest in sewing to own a fabric store, but it certainly makes you more effective in helping customers. Your hobby can actually give you a leg up on come of the competition, particularly if your rival retailers are large chain stores. Many of them have a tough time these days, perhaps because they hire employees who don't sew, and don't know or care about the fabrics in the store. Who better to sell fabric, in a retail store, or by mail order, than someone who loves it?

Mail Order Fabric Sales

Fabric, machines, accessories and notions have all provided stepping stones for the development of the businesses in this chapter.

Lorie Graff of Seattle found a place in this area by combining her dual interests in sewing and belly dancing. This led her to a successful retail and mail order fabric business that today boasts customers all over the country.

In the early 1970's, when belly dancing was gaining in popularity, a co-worker in the municipal court where Graff was administrator talked her into joining a group of others in their office in a ten-week dance class. At the end of the session, of the original group only Graff and the person who was eventually to become her business partner were still in the class. She went on to take more ten-week sessions for the next three years, at the end of which she had earned her teaching certificate in this exotic Eastern art. For the next ten years, Lorie performed professionally and taught, still keeping her day job as court administrator.

During this time, Graff and her friend **Jean Wood**, also of Seattle, together developed patterns for costumes. They were different from anything found in the commercial pattern books at the time (or now, for that matter). She and Jean shared a background in home economics, which gave them skills in design and patternmaking. They did a brisk business among their students, and through mail order, but finding fabrics was still a problem. Knocking on the doors of many fabric reps, Lorie finally found one who would take her seriously. She took a sample of some fabric to a class, and "the students went wild", she says. Jehlor Fantasy Fabrics was born.

Marketing through mail order has consistently accounted for 50% of Graff's business, which she bought wholly from Wood in 1988. "We took a narrow slice out of the fabric retailer's pie," she says. "We saw other stores try to be everything to everyone, and go out of business in the process. We wanted to specialize in dance, all kinds of dance needs." Now in a 3,500 square foot retail space in Seattle, Jehlor ("JEan and LORie, with an H thrown in for the Heck of it"), serves not only belly dancers, but folk dancers, skaters, and companies that make Vegas and Reno show costumes. Diane Shur, the jazz vocalist, and Olympic silver medal skater Rosalind Sumner are two of Graff's many customers. Keeping on top of the dancers' needs is a full-time job for Graff, who is constantly on the lookout for new things. She subscribes to many dance publications, and she gets helpful information from her very creative customers. "This is such a stimulating place to work; I was really getting burned out with my job in the court, seeing so many negative things all day long," she says.

Retail Fabric Store

When we met **Joyce Hittesdorf** in Chapter 4, her dressmaking business was in an office space in Carmel, Indiana. Meanwhile, since other local stores have either gone out of business, or stopped carrying the finer fabrics Hittesdorf's clientele needed, she eventually began carrying quite a selection. Since then, Joyce has expanded her business to include retail fabrics, and moved everything into a freestanding store in Indianapolis, called "Something Wonderful!".

Since the store opened in early fall 1994, Hittesdorf says the store is doing well. She offers a carefully chosen selection of mostly natural fabrics, grouped in color stories. This allows her customers to coordinate their wardrobes better, and makes for more volume sales. Something Wonderful! also cater to local dressmakers, who are encouraged to send in customers to order fabric. Joyce and **Mike Hittesdorf** offer dressmakers a generous incentive to do this: when her customer buys yardage for a project, the dressmaker is given a 20% credit which she can apply as real money towards purchases for herself. Something Wonderful! writes the amount off as advertising, and the dressmaker can "buy" fabric for herself virtually cost-free.

The Hittesdorfs are conscientious about staying away from the dressmaker's customer, and everyone wins. "We don't want to cannibalize our clients' customers," says Mike. Their own custom business shares space in the back portion of the store.

About half of their sales originate from their own custom clothing business and the sale of special order fabrics. The rest is either for special orders for other clothiers, or "walk out" clientele. The special order business is great, according to Mike. It reduces the need to carry lots of inventory, and reduces the overhead of the business, but still brings in a nice profit.

Two additional business boosters are sewing classes and a quarterly newsletter. Joyce includes the other custom sewing pros in the mailings. Tidbits of information about the various fabrics in the store, new patterns and accessories, and calendars of events stimulate interest and draw the customers into the store.

Buying Fabrics

Joyce Hittesdorf goes to wholesale fabric shows, and also makes buying trips to New York. Her most efficient way of buying fabric, though, is through reps of various companies, who visit her shop with samples. Store owners everywhere rely on reps for help on what is selling well elsewhere, new products, timing seasonal purchases, and coordinating choices across different lines at the most attractive price points.

Every company has a slightly different policy, but usually you can expect to find a dollar or "piece" minimum. Most companies require you to purchase at least $100 or at least 10-15 yards, depending on the fabric. In order to carry a good selection of colors and fabrications, make a minimum investment in many fabrics. The dates of each delivery are important; a May delivery of Christmas fabric, for instance would only tie up valuable cash resources; the pattern might also look like just that same old thing to your customer. Time woolens' delivery close to cold weather, and lightweight summery fabrics to warm days.

Most companies allow you to buy C.O.D. until you have established credit with them. Then many companies accept major credit cards. Factoring is ideal for fabric stores. As the go-between, the factor prequalifies you financially, then collects the money and pays the supplier. Once factored, nearly every supplier will deal with you.

You might also deal with suppliers of notions and patterns. Some of the notions' companies will keep track of what you have and replenish your stock as needed. Be aware, though, that they may weigh the "required" stock most heavily in favor of their own profit, not yours. When you let other people spend your money in this fashion you need to watch them carefully.

From Publishing to Mail Order Fabric Sales

Kathy Sandmann began selling fabric by mail order in an unusual way: articles in her home sewing newsletters, *Sewing Sampler* and *Children's Sampler*, mentioned various fabrics. Her readers wrote to ask where they find them, and so Kathy began to list a limited number of choices in her newsletters. In this case, a business began as one thing and changed focus entirely. The mail order fabric sales took over, and now dominate Sandmann's business.

"It's hard to prevent a business from growing," says Kathy. "If you have a good service, or desirable merchandise, it expands." After four years of selling the fabrics and newsletters from her home, Kathy had outgrown her own capabilities. It was imperative to hire help, and she no longer wanted the business in her house in Springfield, Minnesota. Two years in an office space was followed by a move to her current location in a storefront. "You think you can control your size and still be in business, but sometimes you can't keep your customers happy that way. Long-term planning is the important part of the equation." Sandmann feels she wouldn't be in business today if she hadn't been willing to grow with it, though it wasn't an easy process to go through.

Finding Advice

Sandmann's best help and advice came from her local Small Business Development Center. They help her set up her initial bookkeeping system, actually coming to her shop to advise her, and were helpful in creating her business plan. The SBDC can also work with a business owner to find financing. "They can't go to the bank for you, but they can call the bank beforehand and pave the way," Kathy says. For startup businesses, they also help decide which ideas will work best.

Increasing Orders

One of Sandmann's best moves was to install an 800 phone number. Until she moved from her home, she didn't take phone orders, but now she strongly recommends them for mail order success. Her 800 service paid for itself easily. Another avenue to sales that's been getting a good response is an online catalogue mart on the Internet. It will be interesting to see how services like this affect mail order in the coming technological explosion.

Clotilde

"If, ten years ago, you'd told me I'd be where I am today, I'd have said you were smoking those funny cigarettes." This is how **Clotilde** describes the success she's enjoyed with the company that bears her name. But it took a long time to get where she is.

After sewing all her life, Clotilde decided to take commercial pattern drafting classes in Cincinnati, not far from Miami University where she was working on her degree in fashion. Her original goal was a job as in department store buying. Her Home Economics teacher was of the "rip it out" school, and Clotilde suffered her only "C" in college, and switched her major to English! Later, this rich background in sewing came in handy when she worked in the wardrobe department of 20th Century Fox studios for two years.

In the early 1970's, Clotilde informally taught sewing to friends. "I was petrified, until I realized I knew 90% more than anyone else there" Then a local fabric store retailer asked her to teach for him. Clotilde soon saw the magic of teaching – "I love the excitement of seeing how their faces lit up when my students are learning something new," she says. "You can see the light bulbs turn on all over the room." She often showed new products and how to use them, which retailers weren't doing consistently at the time.

One day while visiting the wholesale district of Los Angeles, she noticed some corsage pins. Long and sharp, and with large heads, she thought they would make great sewing pins for her classes. Clotilde began her distributor career with these pins; the owner of the fabric store bought them from her because he didn't want to go to the trouble of buying them. The Iron-All, a forerunner of the current Iron Safe, was her next product. When she found the manufacturer in Van Nuys, she was so enthusiastic about the product that they asked her to be a distributor. Instead, Clotilde said she'd be a rep. She soon found out, though, that retailers would "pat me on the back, and say 'We only buy from a distributor'. Distributors," she quickly learned, "Are order takers, not salespeople. They give you the best price on what they themselves bought at a good price. They stock recognized products that they can buy cheap – not necessarily the newest, or the best for the needs of the buyer."

While she realized Iron-All needed to be shown at trade shows, the manufacturer didn't have the money to pay for a booth for this purpose. So instead Clotilde told all her classes to "nag your fabric store to get this product." As she went along, she found other unusual notions to add to her catalogue, which was just a sheet of paper at the time. After she wrote *Sew Smart*, she began traveling across the country on speaking tours. Demonstrating products not found locally, she began to build a customer base.

By this time, Clotilde had remarried, to her high school sweetheart, and had moved from Los Angeles to Jamestown, Ohio. Her new husband, **Don Lampe**, had a machine tool shop. He gave her a couple of shelves there; soon she was taking over more and more of the shop. When she shipped 50 orders in one week, they had a party. Don asked her what she wanted to do, and she said she wanted the business to grow. Pretty soon Don's office manager was working for Clotilde nights and weekends. Before long, Don sold his business and they moved to Florida. "Don said we'd go to Florida for five years, then move back to California. However, we never left Florida, because by that time, my business had grown too large to move." They started in a small building, with Don, Clotilde, and one employee. Clotilde would come home from seminars, change clothes, and begin packing orders. "To save money, we used old newspapers as packing material."

Clotilde says Don's business experience, along with her seminars and books were the magic combination. It must be: they've gone from the modest beginning of a mere order sheet, to a 100-page catalogue that goes to nearly two million people each year. In addition, she travels an average of 30 weeks a year to the many consumer shows around the country teaching her popular classes. In 1995, for instance, her schedule called for her to be home only two days between mid-September and mid-November. "I couldn't do this if I had children at home," she says. "Or if I didn't have Don – he handles the business while I'm on the road."

Clotilde attends the Direct Marketing Association's National Catalogue Conference, which she feels has been very helpful. The conference, which alternates between Chicago and New York, costs $950, but is worth the money. "The best part is the networking I do there," she says.

Nancy's Notions, Ltd.

Nancy Zieman is busy. Her most visible role is as the host of her own PBS-TV show, "Sewing With Nancy," but she is also president of Nancy's Notions. The company's colorful, 164-page notions' catalogue includes chatty notes on some of the products (in Zieman's own handwriting), a hallmark of the publication since its humble, one-page beginning in 1979. Her catalogue now goes twice-yearly to over 650,000 customers. Nancy has also written several books on fitting, pattern alteration, and helpful sewing hints.

Armed with a degree in Textiles & Clothing from the University of Wisconsin - Stout, Zieman began a job as home economist for Minnesota Fabrics in 1975. She had taken additional sewing training from Ruth Oblander, and when her job at Minnesota Fabrics ended, Oblander asked Nancy to work as her assistant. Co-authoring *The Sew/Fit Manual* was part of her responsibilities.

When her husband Rich, whom she had met and married while working for Minnesota Fabrics, was transferred to northern Minnesota in 1979, Nancy couldn't find a job. She began freelance teaching sewing to extension services and vocational schools afforded. From the beginning, Nancy demonstrated new products to her students, taking orders from her original flyer, a single, two-sided and photocopied page. She began compiling a mailing list from her class rosters, and Nancy's Notions was born. In 1983, on the advice of her accountant, they incorporated the company to become Nancy's Notions, Ltd.

In 1981, Zieman made a 4-week pilot program about sewing for a cable TV station. It worked well, and the producer asked her if she wanted to co-own the show. "In ignorance, or bliss, I said yes," she says. Cable was then in its infancy, and there were only about 3,000,000 viewers in the whole country. Nancy decided TV teaching would be a nice way to limit travel time. This was especially important to her by 1983 when her oldest son, Ted, was born. Around the same time, she and Rich opened her first warehouse, and by 1983 he joined her company.

"Sewing With Nancy"

At first, Nancy's Notions was the only sponsor of "Sewing With Nancy". Soon after the series began, however, the German sewing machine company Pfaff got a new president, a European who had only been in the US for about a month. Nancy approached their ad agency company about Pfaff becoming the second sponsor, and "maybe because the price was right", when the president heard the idea he liked it. This opened the door for other sponsors, and in the next couple of years Gingher Scissors, The McCall Pattern Company, and Freudenberg Pellon all added their names to the opening credits of the show. In 1993, with some changes in public television, "Sewing With Nancy" also added *Sew News* and Signature Threads as sponsors.

"Sewing With Nancy" was on cable for several years; since 1987 it's been seen exclusively on PBS-TV. A marketing plan to work more closely with public TV and strengthen their foothold is underway. Competition from similar shows makes this part of their program important. "Sewing With Nancy" has longevity, though: it's the longest running sewing show on TV.

As offshoots of her seminars and the TV program, Zieman has compiled and summarized the information into several books. She says people seem to like having an augmentation to a class, something for later reference. Similarly, they have arranged video excerpts from the shows by category. Her book *Let's Sew!* was commissioned by the National 4-H Council for use as the basic information book for beginning sewing, and is now in use in at least 22 states.

Nancy says "One of my strongest points, I think, is that I'm a good teacher." TV brought sewing into the homes of many who had never sewn before; the books and videos have gone even further to dispense sewing information. She feels sewing is gaining momentum, although it may never be like it was in the 70's. "People say to me: I watch your show... but I don't sew. I have to chuckle about that!"

Delegating Authority

Nancy Zieman credits her incredible success in so many different areas to her "very excellent staff". Over 130 employees take orders, field questions from customers (even non-customers), help with the TV show, make samples, assist with her many books, and produce the twice-yearly catalogue. "Because I started this business by myself, and worked alone for several years, I often feel the best person to do something is me. It's hard to let go. But I have lots of ideas roaming around in my mind, and if I can spread them around, everyone does a better job." Her employees seem to like this approach. They are also amazed that Nancy remembers the names of everyone, even new hires.

On planning Zieman says "Sometimes the tail does wag the dog, and then I have to sit back, reevaluate and prioritize." She admires her husband Rich for his planning ability: "I'm not a great planner, my husband is much better. He can look at things 3-5 years ahead. I admire his great outlook." Nancy feels her strength in this area is her flexibility; if something isn't working, she changes it immediately.

One change the company has made recently was to build its own 50,000 square foot warehouse facility. They had been renting space for several years and then it became unavailable. Now they have consolidated all their operations under one enormous roof: offices, warehouse, mail order fulfillment, and a 4,000 square foot, retail fabric store, Pfaff dealership, and classroom area. Employees say the facility is the cleanest they have ever worked in, and the most comfortable. Even the warehouse is air-conditioned. They planned for expansion when they built this facility: space for a second floor was incorporated into the design to minimize the costs of adding on later. This makes good business sense, as the company expanded three times between 1990 and 1995.

In the past, Nancy's Notions has hosted a Sewing Weekend Expo® for sewing enthusiasts from all over the country in April.

Beginning in 1996 it will take place in May because the April date conflicted with other industry events. About 3,000 people participate, with 200-600 in each class. Students are bused to auditoriums to hear name speakers, then bused back to the Nancy's Notions, Ltd. complex for shopping. To accommodate so many customers at once, employees move the entire fabric store's contents to the warehouse during the weekend.

Retail Sewing Machine Sales

Like Joyce Hittesdorf, **Londa Rohlfing** successfully combined a dressmaking business with a retail store for four years. While Londa sells fabric and heirloom sewing supplies, she realized her bread and butter is her Elna and Pfaff sewing machine dealership. She feels she couldn't make a success of her shop without the machines. Since then, Londa has slimmed her operation down to sell machines and fabrics only.

According to Rohlfing, pricier machines require more service to the customer, and better training. She loves selling Elnas and Pfaffs, as she feels as they are the most user-friendly of the various brands. Her store both sells and services machines. Both companies have repair training classes for their dealers, and Londa took advantage of this training for her staff. Customers are more willing to buy machines if they know the same store can also repair and service them. This is important, as competition is stiff. "You'd be lucky these days to get a keystone price on machines; more and more machine dealers have to discount," Rohlfing says. Keystone is a doubling of the wholesale price, which can be substantial on today's higher priced machines.

Rohlfing also offers many classes in her shop. A nationally known sewing teacher, Londa teaches heirloom sewing techniques, embellishment, silk ribbon embroidery, and several basic to advanced sewing topics. A move to a much larger store in 1995 (1,300 square feet to 6,000 square feet) has helped accommodate her classes.

Advertising

Rohlfing says the success of a shop can be very dependent on the coverage by local media. How editors and writers feel about you and your business can make or break it. Londa emceed the fashion show for a local charity luncheon for years. Her duties there gave her a public face, aside from the charity work she felt strongly about. One experiment that didn't work was to organize a 3-hour remote broadcast of a local radio show in her shop. $2,000 later, she realized it was not a very good idea. Direct mailing is by far the best use of Londa's advertising dollar; she occasionally purchases the *Sew News* mailing list for her area, with good results. She cautions "Some who would do this might be tempted to use it more than once. There are dummies included in one-time mailing lists, which alert the seller if you use the list more than once." Londa also says having a Christian-based business guides these business practices.

Starting Up

As part of a house restoration he was doing, **Michael Murphy** took estimates for some slipcovers, and draperies for three windows. A national discount department store gave him a price of $3,700. Michael decided a sewing machine would quickly pay for itself, so he bought a Singer. "I was captivated almost instantly," he says. He found sewing hypnotic and meditative, but decided he needed something more challenging, so he bought some simple patterns to make clothing for himself. This wasn't as much fun, until he learned to fit himself.

After reading everything he could find on sewing, Michael enrolled in the Fashion Institute of Technology's (FIT) small business program, and began taking pattern drafting and other sewing-related courses. Part of a class project was to make a business plan, and Murphy chose to make his on a sewing machine store. He joined the International Sewing Machine Dealer's Association (ISMDA), and went to meetings for a couple of years, while still employed in his job as Chief of Information Systems for an online data systems company. More and more, he felt he wanted to do something with people rather than with corporations. "I no longer wanted to feign enthusiasm for what I was doing at work," he says.

In order to lay the groundwork for eventually owning his own store, Michael took a job in a Singer store in Elizabeth, New Jersey, where he learned to teach, and to repair and sell machines. "You have to prove to manufacturers that you know about being in business," Murphy says. His membership in the trade association helped with this, giving him credibility as to his seriousness.

"I decided I wanted a fiber art focus to my store, with no ugly hardware edges," Michael says. At first, he wasn't interested in selling vacuum cleaners, a side line for many dealers. He has since changed his mind: "More people vacuum than sew, and vacuum cleaner repair can bring in cash flow." Other inventory items that Michael considered when making his business plan were parts and accessories, patterns, notions, knitting machines, looms and spinning wheels. He planned to have classes using the latter to spur sales. Having other fiber arts equipment in his store made him different from the other two stores in Kingston, New York. "The store should reflect customers' passion for their hobby, and they should insist that the person they are buying from knows what they are selling. When someone comes into my shop, I consider myself a facilitator, and help them find a machine that fits their hobby. Also, manufacturers want you to be able to afford enough of their line so the customer can trade up or down."

What to Expect

Murphy says after a few years in business, a store owner can expect to make $35,000-50,000 a year, depending on their location and how well they run their business. With more stores, the figure goes higher. He recommends that anyone opening such a store know their retail math. He took courses to learn about profit and loss, balance sheets, and open-to-buy. Markups are especially important in a retail store with the attendant overhead of renting space, Yellow Pages ads, and hiring employees. Classes help generate interest in the merchandise, and can mean the difference between a store succeeding and failing. As Murphy's old boss once told him: "We owe it to our customers to remain profitable."

Chapter 24

Teaching: Children and Adults

Sewing classes in school curricula are relatively rare these days. Traditional, and once mandatory, clothing construction courses have been replaced by what are perceived as more critically needed 90's subjects such as parenting, drug and alcohol abuse prevention, and more stringent academic subjects. If you can effectively communicate your body of sewing knowledge, the rewards can be great. Of all the areas of specialization in sewing, teaching can be one of the most profitable. Also, don't let the lack of a home economics degree keep you from turning your talents to a career in teaching.

Getting Started

Getting started requires planning and effort on three fronts. First you must decide what to teach. Beginning sewing is a good place to test the waters, and draws from the largest group of students. For the same reasons that alterations and custom sewing services are thriving, people want to learn to make better fitting, higher quality clothing for themselves or others. Other options include tailoring, quilting, and a variety of sewn crafts and home decorating projects. You'll need lesson plan that outlines the information you would like to present in class. Second, you must decide where to teach, and third, you must attract students. Fabric stores and sewing machine dealerships are good places to fulfill these last two requirements.

To help others who want to teach, Cheri Sizemore of Texas produced a lesson plan for two levels of beginning sewing. Her approach was to have students make sample garments illustrating the techniques she demonstrated. The pupil could then make a real, wearable garment at the same time at home, on her own. The ½-scale sample garment then served as a reference for future sewing projects. (See Sources.)

Partnership with Fabric Stores

Nancy Gray says "Fabric stores have given me unbelievable support". She had talked with store managers for several years about teaching before she actually opened her Mission Viejo, California school. Their input and encouragement led her to believe that she could make a success of such an endeavor. Gray uses a lesson plan adapted from the one used by Cheri Sizemore. However, Gray's uses a slightly different approach. Where Sizemore had all her students sew the same sample garment, Nancy has her pupils choose from toddler and child-sized patterns. Then, when students finish the course section, she offers them the opportunity of either keeping the finished garments, or donating them to a local homeless shelter.

Once Gray's students have made a project or two, they generally graduate to commercial patterns. She encourages those in her classes to choose patterns incorporating as many of the techniques they learned in the sample garment as possible. Nancy alters the patterns if needed, so the students can concentrate on learning the techniques. "First, the garment has to look great, or they'll get discouraged," she says. "They need to make something that appeals to them, that gets them excited about sewing." Nancy teaches industrial shortcuts wherever she can, and has created a blend of different methods. "My philosophy is that there's no right way or wrong way; there are lots of different ways."

In Gray's home studio she has set up five complete sewing stations. Each machine has a basket nearby with all the latest notions. "I try to keep up with the new technology." Two heights of cutting tables and an adjustable ironing station serve both child and adult students. One table has a serger that everyone in the class takes turns using.

Class Scheduling

"I have to set up my classes for how families live these days," Nancy Gray says. "Kids are begging their parents for sewing lessons, but they're in so many activities." She currently teaches four classes a day: an adult class in the morning, then another in the evening, and two children's classes after school, back to back. Each class is 1½ hours long, which Gray says works well with her and with her students. Her biggest problem right now is serving all the prospective students who want to learn. There just isn't enough of Nancy to go around, and she has a full waiting list. "Some of my students just keep taking classes."

In the small community near Waterloo, Iowa where **Beki Biesterfelt** lives, the pool of students is smaller. Beki tries to attract a different group of students each month, though. She provides a variety of classes to reflect the wide interest range of her pupils. "Some people who sew are crafters; some people who sew are quilters; and some people sew clothes, too" she says. She enjoys beginners the most. "They're so enthusiastic, so willing to learn." Her attempts to vary the structure of her classes has led to some unusual techniques, such as having students spatter-paint white fabric outdoors, making each of their garments unique.

Teaching in a local fabric store was a frustrating experience for **Nancy Marden**. While the owner of the store supplied machines for her classes, they were low-end models of the brands carried there. If a student wished to bring her own, top-of-the-line competing brand, the store owner was understandably unhappy. Also, Marden had trouble with students forgetting equipment at a crucial class, like a foot pedal or a zipper foot.

Gradually, most of Nancy's classes have moved to a space in the same building as her Lewiston, Maine apartment. She prefers this, because she doesn't "have to load up everything and drag it over there" for each class at the store. Other pluses: the "aggravation factor is lower", and she doesn't have to share her fee with the store owner. Also, when pupils ask for her advice on machines, she can honestly advise them without bias. She generally suggests buying a lower end machine first; this way they can see if they enjoy sewing enough to invest in a more costly machine. She tells students that good basics are more important than the bells and whistles on the higher priced models. "They can always trade up," she explains, adding "If they can't understand a complicated machine, they get too frustrated to continue sewing."

As a left-hander, Marden feels she has an advantage in teaching – as long as right-handed students stand in front of her. In the case of other lefties, she has them stand beside or behind her while she demonstrates detailed processes.

The motivating factor behind her decision to teach was money; she wanted to be paid for her sewing knowledge. She already has a full-time job, as the manager of three fabric departments in her family's chain of discount stores in the Northeast. "That gives me a guaranteed weekly paycheck and a health insurance policy," she says. Nancy has lots of energy. In addition to her 40-hour week at Marden's, she also teaches and sews for others another 50-60 hours each week!

Because Lewiston is a mill town in an economically depressed area, it's difficult to charge the prices that Nancy would like to command. Having a regular salary allows her to do what she loves, while keeping her prices affordable to the local public.

Giving her students the chance to tell her what they want out of the course is a hallmark of a Nancy Marden class. Particularly, she asks students who have sewn before what they want to learn. "I could throw darts at a dartboard all night long without hitting anything, otherwise." She says she asks them "You've paid $40 for four weeks of this class; what do you want to know?" In recent classes, one person learned to tailor a jacket, working on fusibles and fitting. Another student, a fellow Maine Dressmaker's Guild member, learned to make a wedding gown. This individual, though she works with handicapped children, decided she didn't have the patience to make another!

Teaching Children

Six years ago, **Carol Hawkey** began teaching children to sew. After a year of frustration with the children's patterns she was using, she drafted a series of her own. Carol developed "Directions" patterns for children who can read to teach themselves to sew. Using these in her classes has helped her to refine them. She says she has her pupils read the instructions, then ask for help. "I'm there to guide them, and to identify potential problems, not to tell them where to put each stitch."

Her patterns' instructions begin after the machine is threaded, as she feels this task is somewhat difficult for children to master at first. Kids' fine motor skills are not as well developed as their large motor functions. It is actually harder for very young children to sew by hand than with a machine. Hawkey starts children in her classes at age 7, which she also recommends to those buying her patterns. She

offers these clues to whether or not a child is ready to learn to sew
with a machine:

- Can the child write his or her name neatly?

- Is she able to color within the lines?

- Can the child remember a string of simple instructions?

Nancy Gray and Nancy Marden both teach children, as well as
adults. While Gray starts kids at age 8, Marden prefers to teach
preteens and up. Marden says of teaching children: "To expect
perfection from little kids is not reasonable". She also says that, at
the end of an adult class, she's "mentally brain dead" from students
"picking my brain"; she gets tired physically from teaching children.
You have to keep alert in a kids' class; so many things can happen
quickly with all that dangerous equipment around.

Islander School of Fashion Arts

A 1500 square foot building currently houses the Islander School
of Fashion Arts, Inc. **Margaret Islander**, a nationally known
instructor in factory sewing methods, realized her dream when she
opened her school in Grants Pass, Oregon in 1979. It's not unusual
for 125 students a semester to enroll in her classes. Her experience as
a technician at a training center for garment industry workers gave
her the background necessary to teach others a faster, pinless way to
sew. Even stitchers with many years of experience can learn to sew
better with Islander's methods. Her friendly, approachable manner
makes her instruction even more accessible. Margaret has expanded
her courses into videos, with the hope that technology would help
her reach an even greater audience. (See Chapter 25)

Quilting Classes

A deep love of quilting inspired **Jenell Noeth** to share her
knowledge with others. With a maximum of eight in a class, Noeth
teaches how to cut strips with rotary cutters, and piece them on a
machine. Her interest began ten years ago, when she took a class and
saw how the rotary cutters simplified the tedious process of cutting
pieces. Quilting is enjoying a revival in many areas of the country,
providing an opportunity for you to teach, if this is your interest.

In January 1993, Jenell began augmenting her income by
teaching others to piece and quilt. She holds classes twice a month,

and has an average of four students in each class, and a maximum of eight. Her classes draw from the surrounding communities of Kansas City and Shawnee, and response has been very good. While teaching from her home is fine for now, Jenell's ultimate goal is to open a shop selling fabrics, with enough space for more in-depth classes. This will allow her to expand the line of quilting fabrics she now carries, and will offer her a larger, more private space for classes.

The Traveling Classroom

Also capitalizing on the current craze for quilts, **Patsy Shields** travels around the country teaching quilt embellishment and appliqué. After a serger seminar she attended given by Sue Green for the Tacony Corporation, Patsy asked Sue how she could get started doing the same job. Green told her who to contact at Tacony, the manufacturer of Babylock machines. Soon, Sulky of America asked Patsy to give her nationwide seminars for them, as well.

Traveling from her Indiana home "at least 150 days a year", Patsy has machine arts, serger, heirloom sewing, and pants and blazer fitting seminars in her repertoire. As a freelance educator, "I work for whoever needs me"; she makes her own schedule. On behalf of Sulky of America, the various dealers contact her to line up her popular talks. This kind of teaching is not an ongoing dialogue with a group of students, but it can provide a very good living. The lecture circuit used to be busy only during certain seasons, but it has gotten pretty steady, according to Shields.

When Patsy knows she is going to be lecturing in a particular area of the country, she tries to "piggyback" other talks in the same region. This is especially helpful when Tacony schedules her for one of their dealers. Doing her own marketing allowed her the leeway and freedom to recently add a publisher as one of her sponsors. Having booths at quilt shows, the American Sewing Guild consumer shows, and trade shows like the Independent Sewing Machine Dealers Association show, have helped Patsy spread the word about her services. She has also attended the In Stitches consumer show, and the Louisville Quilt Festival as an exhibitor.

A job with White/Elna machine company required **Jan Saunders** to begin her teaching career. Her book, *Speed Sewing*, summed up the high points of these seminars. (See Chapter 25.) When Book of the Month Club chose this book as a club selection, Jan began lecturing nationwide for Chilton, who published it. A happy, unexpected result was that she enjoyed herself *and* made money.

Seminars as a Business

Based on the success of the seminars she'd been giving, Jan saw another business opportunity. She could teach the topics of not only her own books, but those of other Chilton authors, as well. It would promote the books, while she taught consumers how to improve their sewing techniques and use new products that were coming out. "I wanted to help the wholesalers by giving them a more direct line to the consumer." She now supervises sewing instructors all over the country who are teaching material found in Chilton books.

Though she had to take out loans to get started, Jan says it's been a great experience. In order to lessen the liability risk of her seminars, in case someone tripped on a cord, etc., she decided to incorporate. "It's more expensive this way, but it gives me a peaceful feeling, and I feel more professional. I've always run my business as a business, and this is part of being a pro." It also gives her more credibility with potential clients. This attitude extends to maintaining her home office as an arena for doing business, as well. "I don't try to take care of my son during business hours. He goes to day care while I'm working, but having my own business allows me more flexibility to be with him."

Describing her goals for "Speed Sewing Ltd.", Jan envisions servicing the home sewing industry. "No one else is showing consumers how to use products". Manufacturers might utilize Jan's staff to educate their customers, thereby improving their sales, and providing a customer service. A word of advice to others with aspirations in a sewing-related business: "You have to be out there shaking the bushes all the time; you have to be passionate about what you're doing".

Chapter 25

Writing, Video Production, Pattern Publication, Consumer Shows

Many of the names mentioned in this chapter will be familiar to the readers of this book. These people have turned their knowledge of sewing subject into readily accessible information for the sewing public, generally the home sewing public.

Two or three decades ago, people learned to sew from their mothers and grandmothers (occasionally from grandfathers), with skills passing down through the generations like a family lore. Then, when the sixties and seventies saw many stay-at-home persons take up careers, and families became more scattered geographically, the hitherto free flow of sewing intelligence slowed to a mere trickle.

The computer age of the late eighties and nineties revived the surge of information, and contributed heavily to the concentrated mass of sewing data, but the carrier changed from Mother to mass media. The magazines *Sew News* and *Threads* both started at about the same time, as did the American Sewing Guild and Nancy Zieman's popular TV show, "Sewing with Nancy." A look back to that era also shows the independent creation of several professional sewing groups across the country. This growing awareness of sewing techniques, tools and information fostered a climate ripe for the many books written in this period. At the same time, several specialized newsletters have become successful, as well.

From Teaching to Writing – Claire Shaeffer

The grand lady of sewing books is **Claire Shaeffer**. Her books have added significantly to the knowledge of today's sewing enthusiasts. From a former bathroom in her Palm Springs home, Claire has pounded out more than a dozen books, and was the first to simplify and adapt industrial techniques for the home sewing market.

Shaeffer began teaching general garment construction courses at the College of the Desert in 1975. Since Claire had industrial training, the college purchased overlock machines (then only available for the industry), industrial sewing machines, and some professional ironing systems, for the students' use. Though her classes were in a traditional home ec program, the curriculum allowed students to transfer to other schools, including trade schools. Because home sewing methods of the time really looked like home sewing, Claire wanted to show her classes how to get more professional results. She began to adapt industrial techniques to the home sewing methods in use at the time.

In 1976, Shaeffer was in a serious auto accident requiring a long convalescence. Since many of her other activities were curtailed, she wrote a book based on the course handouts she'd been using. This first book, *101 Sewing Shortcuts*, was self-published. Claire advertised in many publications – her best response came from Vogue Pattern Magazine, she says. However, she was more inclined to write additional books than to promote the one she'd written. "Publishing companies have better access to distribution channels than writers do."

Because she hated the self-publishing process, Claire sent the book to Sterling Publishing Company. It became *The Complete Book of Sewing Shortcuts*, and hit the bookstores in 1981. "At the time, pattern companies didn't want to deviate from the party line of home sewing techniques," she says. "They still don't, but some machine techniques, such as the 'stitch in the ditch' method, are now included in pattern guidesheets. Even in a $500 man's shirt the only handstitching you'll see is in the buttons, and very occasionally the buttonholes." It made sense to her to use the faster, more efficient industry methods at home, and her books show adaptations of these techniques to the traditional methods used by the pattern companies.

Meanwhile, Claire returned to the College of the Desert. When she began teaching an alterations class there she wanted to give students a definitive method to price alterations, but found there wasn't one. Using price lists she'd collected over 20 years from all over the country, she put together a pricing method widely used today. *Price it Right*, the 18-page result of her research, was also self-published as a booklet in 1986.

When Claire and her husband Charlie bought their Palm Springs home in 1976, there was a sunken tub in a separate 10' X 12' room off one of the many bathrooms. Since it wasn't very practical for her lifestyle, Claire had the fittings taken off (leaving the plumbing for a future owner), and had the tub covered over with a carpeted platform. The existing marble counter running the length of the room serves as a desk for a computer, printer, and other paraphernalia. The breathtaking view of the nearby San Jacinto mountains reflected in the upper windows provides ample inspiration.

About her actual writing process, Shaeffer says she does her best work first thing in the morning (after taking advantage of her western time zone to make less expensive long distance calls). Sometimes she writes all afternoon when a deadline looms. Experiments with sewing techniques at the machine occasionally interrupt the writing process. Claire usually holds her outline in her head, rather than on paper, and she writes and edits her work simultaneously. She defines herself as a "linear writer", preferring to write from beginning to end.

Shaeffer's latest books include a pair of books on the various types of pockets, a return to her roots with a textbook on industrial sewing techniques, and the critically acclaimed *Couture Sewing Techniques*. To research her couture book Claire read several books in their original French to get a true sense of their topic. She owns one of the largest collections of books on sewing in this country: "I began buying them when we moved to Palm Springs, where it was difficult to get many of the books I wanted, even on inter-library loan. I picked them up wherever I found them. My collection of sewing books is better than the one at the Fashion Institute of Design and Marketing." She feels that reading these books helped her develop the broad information base she drew from when studying couture collections. An extensive collection of couture clothing bought at secondhand stores all over the country adds to Shaeffer's incredibly rich store of knowledge in this specialty sewing area.

Gail Brown

Another prolific sewing writer is **Gail Brown,** who has written since she was 22. Her books are aimed at a slightly different audience, with emphasis on serging and other quick techniques. *Sewing With Sergers*, one of Brown's has sold over 700,000 copies. She credits this book's phenomenal success to three things: it was one of the first books to demystify the then-new serger; it was priced right; and the instruction books that originally came with Japanese-made sergers were poorly translated and incomplete. Gail hastened to add "I don't make $1 a book, by the way!"

"I write, that's what I do. I don't travel; I write every day," says Brown. She stands out as an author who rarely attends trade or consumer shows. Though Gail lives in the tiny town of Hoquiam, Washington, using faxes, modems, and telephones, she can stay at home and work for anyone. And Gail is very much a child of the electronic age. One of the first sewing experts to venture online in a big way, she has made a thorough exploration of many of the services the Internet offers. She credits much of today's better information flow to the accessibility of both printed and electronically published data.

Brown knew she wanted to teach sewing while she was in college, and when she graduated, she went to New York City to do so. From there, she took a marketing job with a fabric company specializing in double knits, increasing her fiber knowledge. After a short stint writing menus and packaging for Mr. Steak in Denver, Gail took her "last real job" – as communications manager for Stretch & Sew, overseeing books and patterns.

Pati Palmer and Susan Pletsch, the original partners of Palmer/Pletsch, gave Gail her first opportunity as a writer. "I'll never forget that," she says. "I wasn't as experienced then – I didn't have a business track record at all. They had a lot of confidence in a beginner. People in the industry have also been very good to me. Readers are the best; they're a great bunch to work for. You might think, as a writer, that you don't have a boss, but you do. I'm having an ongoing conversation with my readers each time I write, and must serve their changing needs." It must be working – only one of Brown's books is out of print.

Jan Saunders

While Gail Brown prefers to stay at home and write, some authors enjoy the stimulation of traveling and speaking about their books. Claire Shaeffer makes a few appearances a year; **Jan Saunders** has made a business out of public speaking, in conjunction with her writing (See the previous chapter). The scores of Sew Better Seminars Jan gives every year help promote not only her own books, but many others also published by Chilton.

As a home economist for White/Elna Sewing Machine Company, Jan began teaching seminars at various dealers around the country. It was often frustrating for her, as many of the retailers cared only about turning students into customers. Saunders was more interested in educating the seminar attendees, and soon realized that if she wrote her information down it might be more helpful for the student. A manuscript came out of that conviction, but her frustrations weren't yet over. The first publisher she queried agreed to publish, then lost her manuscript, and eventually asked for their advance back. Jan rewrote the text, they lost it again, and she eventually had to sue to get the manuscript back. *Speed Sewing* was finally published five years after she first wrote it, in 1985, and Jan nervously watched every phase of its production. Who can blame her? She went on a nationwide speaking tour to promote the book, which became a Book of the Month Club selection, and has brought Jan a great deal of satisfaction at last.

When Jan queried editor Robbie Fanning at Chilton about her *Sew, Serge & Press* book, Robbie called her immediately. Not only was she interested in this book, but she'd been looking for a co-author to write the Know Your Machine series with Jackie Dodson. Consumers wanted how-to books that related specifically to their brand of machine, and Jan and Jackie's collaboration was very successful. The pair were invited to give seminars in Florida. The books they took "sold like crazy", which put Jan on the path she now treads, in her successful speaking business.

Video Production

In her 20's, **Margaret Islander** moved to Los Angeles and began studying commercial pattern drafting and grading. Her enthusiasm led to a job as a technical assistant in a training center for garment industry workers. Seeing how much easier industrial methods were, Margaret decided to teach them to the home sewing market. When she moved to Oregon in 1970, she began teaching these techniques at the college level and in other seminars. By 1979, she opened the Islander School of Fashion Arts in its present location in Grants Pass, Oregon.

To further disseminate the information taught in her classes, Islander decided to produce videos. Someone had urged her to do so, arguing that many people have VCRs these days. She found a good professional videographer to do the production work for her, and had a new studio built in her school facilities for this purpose. "It was agony looking at the video the first time," she says, of seeing herself on the screen. The videographer, from Los Angeles, has since moved to Grants Pass, where together they have produced several videos for the home sewing market.

Islander credits some of her initial success to good reviews in *Sew News* and other sewing publications. Professionally produced ads get great results, project a quality image, and coordinate with the other parts of her business. Speaking and showing her products at trade shows have also been tremendous for sales. "The videos are selling well, there's lots of growth," Margaret says. She has published books on Pattern Drafting and Pants Fitting, that sell as an accompaniment to each video, which gives her more to sell at the trade shows. She is often accompanied on the road by her sister, who helps her by tending the booth while Margaret is giving a talk.

Sandra Betzina Webster – Books, Videos, TV

"I was a mother, and all I could do was sew," says **Sandra Betzina Webster**. Using her talents and $600, Sandra opened a small sewing school, the California School of Fashion Dressmaking, which she operated for 8 years. Sandra taught when her children were in bed, and sold the school when she found she was expecting twins. (Webster sold this school to one of her teachers, who in turn sold it to Marcy Tilton, yet another teacher, who renamed it the Sewing Workshop. Linda Lee of Oklahoma now owns the Sewing Workshop.)

Using her credentials as a teacher, Webster began writing a sewing column for the local paper. "This gave me a foot in the door to talk with name sewing experts, companies, and ready-to-wear people." After four years of writing, Sandra sent one of her brochures to local TV stations, asking "What about doing TV segments on sewing?" One said "Yes", and she began taping programs. After two years on the air, she was asked to become the spokesperson for the then-American Home Sewing Association (now American Home Sewing & Craft Association). Her subsequent appearances on talk shows on their behalf gave her further exposure and name recognition.

"Most people wait until everything is perfect; my advice is to go ahead and do it," Webster says. An inheritance of $41,000 gave Sandra the necessary capital to self-publish her first book, *Power Sewing*. "I took a big risk; I had to use all the money." It was a big book, and the art and layout were expensive for her first run of 10,000 copies. Sandra says today desktop publishing would make the process easier. Though her books were selling well, she decided to make videos for two reasons: She wouldn't have to travel as much, and because "some concepts need to be seen." Sandra interviewed 25-30 production people before she found a good fit. Her catalogue now carries 12 video titles and 3 books, and her syndicated column, also called "Power Sewing," appears in newspapers all over the country. Webster's latest venture is her Home & Garden Network TV show, "Sew Perfect", going into its third season in the fall of 1995.

Consumer Shows

At one time or another, everyone profiled in this chapter has participated in either a trade or a consumer show as a way to demonstrate and sell their products. Though there are several show promotion management companies now, as recently as twelve years ago there weren't any privately owned consumer sewing shows in the US.

In Stitches Consulting, Ltd.

In 1987, the stock market collapsed. While that was bad news for many people, it opened a window of opportunity to **Carol Dodge**. Carol had been a stockbroker and financial advisor at a firm in Vancouver, specializing in mutual funds. As a broker, she had won many trips, traveled to conferences for her business, and had arranged seminars for her clients. When the market took a nose dive, Dodge decided she needed a change in her professional life. Because she had been a lifelong sewing enthusiast, she at first thought she would like to open a fabric store. An exploratory trip to the American Home Sewing & Craft Association retail trade show in

San Francisco that year gave her the idea to do a retail-level show. An article in "USA Today", which told of the sales of fabrics, notions and patterns as doubling in the five years before 1991 convinced Dodge that she was onto something she could make a business of. She'd learned a great deal about financing and business startups in her former business, which helped get her started. In Stitches Consulting, Ltd. also drew on Carol's experience with the many conferences she'd set up in her finance career.

In six months, Dodge put together a show in Vancouver and made $10,000 with the event. "Looking back, it was crazy to try to do a show in six months," she now says. "It really takes a year to plan, and eighteen months is a better lead time to feel comfortable with the event." That was in 1987, the second show the next year was even better, as were the two shows she put on in 1989, branching out to include Calgary. In her fourth and fifth years there were competing shows in both Vancouver and Calgary, so Carol began looking for a way to escape competition for such a limited market. That fifth year, in 1992, Dodge expanded into the US, with her first show in Southfield, Michigan. The higher population and interest in sewing drew her to the US, and with good results. In Stitches shows in Arlington, Texas; San Jose and San Diego, California; Philadelphia and Boston have been added to their calendar. When Dodge had a chance to buy a competing show (Make It Myself), she did, adding Chicago, Cleveland, Tampa Atlanta to the roster of cities covered.

Though In Stitches Consulting, Inc. has a tight schedule, with several shows a year, Carol's close-knit staff works like a well-run machine. Everyone has sewing background, along with sales and management experience. Dodge says they have all grown together. The results are tangible: Carol has been nominated three years in a row as Entrepreneurial Woman of the Year.

Dodge attributes her success to three things: "My personal drive to succeed, the people I've met, and my interest in sewing. I've never done anything before I was this passionate about. I don't even think about the money, but somehow it comes. This is fulfilling to me, a real joy." It also takes a great deal of work: a visit to Carol and her staff during a show revealed they had been living in the hotel for almost a week before the event. Each show takes six to eighteen months of solid planning beforehand. They make several visits to each city where shows are scheduled during the planning stages of each show.

Chapter 26

Piecework & Factory Sewing

In spite of the mass exodus of garment manufacturing from the United States to overseas factories, opportunities for flexible small shops abound. For instance, a company that requires a dozen, a hundred, or even thousands of an article often has a difficult time finding a factory to sew them. Such smaller contracts are gravy to the independent shops that have sprung up to fill this need.

Portrait of a Factory Owner

When the character of his employer's business changed, **Jim Dennis** took his twenty years experience in apparel engineering and opened his own contracting company along with his wife, **Doloris**. In the beginning, Ansew's main customer was Jim's former employer, Cincinnati-based Bayless Brothers, makers of Polly Flinders children's clothing. Jim had left Bayless because the company had moved most of their manufacturing operations to the Caribbean. However, small runs such as those needed for sales representative's samples could not be made offshore. Jim's company could make them – usually several hundred samples (2 dozen for each salesperson) for $6-10 apiece.

Because Ansew couldn't keep busy with the needs of just one company, they have taken in other production work. Now they produce a line of hospital wear, making 20 different styles of lab coats they've developed. Because protective clothing is strictly regulated, Ansew has to conform to careful specifications of construction. Other articles they manufacture include raincoats for firefighters, protective clothing for laundry workers, and boot inserts.

For the raincoats, Ansew invested in a $20,000 seam sealing machine. Another machine that allows the item to feed off the arm with a double needle stitch cost almost $65,000.

Their nearly 40 employees work in an airy mini-factory filled with a wide variety of industrial machines. Dennis says "You can't train an operator overnight," and he estimates it takes up to four years for an operator to get up to his or her top sewing speed. Machine operators in his area earn from $8-15 per hour.

According to Jim Dennis, most companies supply what is known as "cutwork" to their subcontractors. This means the garment pieces are precut, ready for assembly. Cutting large quantities of one garment is usually done on an electronic cutting machine, made by Gerber, or one of a couple European companies. Dennis visualizes eventually purchasing one of these machines in order to offer cutting services in addition to the manufacturing. The electronic machines allow up to 90-95% of fabric utilization by plotting out the placement of the various garment pieces along the length of the fabric.

Mini-Factory

In her home in suburban Fairfield, Ohio, **Deborah Jackson** oversees an even smaller version of a factory. With over a dozen industrial machines, Debby assembles an incredible array of garments and goods for her customers.

When Jackson and **Linda Walden** (profiled in Chapter 20) attended a seminar for small business owners, Debby stood up and asked a question. In doing so she explained that she and Linda were sewing for others as partners. A few minutes after she sat down a business card with a note asking her to call made its way to her seat. When they called to find out what this unusual behavior was about, they were asked if they wanted a job repairing several hundred hotel tablecloths. Linda and Debby said yes, not realizing what they were in for. Using two home sewing machines, they patched the salvageable tablecloths, and they cut around holes and rehemmed larger cloths, making them smaller. With the money they made they each bought a faster industrial machine.

Jackson discovered something important in this experience: she enjoyed sewing fast, and not having to think about how something was going to go together or fit. She left the comparative safety of her computer programming job at General Electric so she could work from home and enjoy her new daughter. For a while, she and Walden had a loose partnership, sharing the work in making orders of hundreds of aprons and other jobs. When Linda changed her business focus to embroidery, Debby decided to continue the manufacturing side.

A local uniform company had an order for several hundred maternity pants for their pregnant employees but they weren't equipped to make such a small order. Jackson's Sewing Services bid and won the job. Debby and her helpers inserted maternity panels into the cut pants pieces the client supplied. The only drawback was finding the panels; she finally had to improvise by modifying an existing product that wasn't quite right to make it work. A large order for inserting buttonholes in aprons for a grocery store (for their name tags) prompted Debby to buy a buttonhole machine. It paid for itself right away, not only with this job, but in showing the contractor how well equipped her "factory" was.

Over the years, Jackson has developed methods for attaching trims and bindings, and seaming in the fastest possible ways. She has purchased all her machines from Bob and David Gray, father and son industrial machine dealers, who have many combined years of factory experience. Many of the tips she uses came from their collective wisdom.

Pricing Services

In order to price a job to make money, Debby suggests making a sample first. Time yourself, and notice any places where you might need to shave steps. Realize there will be a learning curve for both you and your employees, and that each project is slightly different. Make all the construction details that can be made on one machine at once, then move to the next process. Jackson uses tray tables to hold batches of pieces to be sewn together. She also says to figure the amount of time you will spend clipping, stacking, folding, counting, boxing, and shipping into the final price of the job. And don't forget the paperwork – these activities take time, too.

The Right Tool for the Job

Jackson further contributes her success to a willingness to use industrial machines. Besides the buttonhole machine, she has several single needle straight stitchers, a double needle machine, industrial sergers, blindstitchers, a needle feed machine, and a bartacker. The needle feed works similarly to a dual-feed mechanism on a domestic machine, and is useful for sewing long stretches of fabrics that might shift with another machine. Because this type of sewing doesn't require much ironing, this workroom has only a household iron.

Piecework

Bob Gray, who sells and services industrial machines in Cincinnati, makes a side business of piecework. He says jobs as simple as constructing pockets for work shirts can be lucrative with the right equipment. Twice yearly, a local uniform company sends him 5,000-6,000 route book pockets to make. Bob demonstrated to the author his pocket making process. He used two machines: a double needle straight stitch, and an overlock machine... and it took 36 seconds! His secret? He invested in a nifty gadget called a pocket press that forms the points for each pocket in 9 seconds. Also, he didn't sit down to sew, but remained standing, giving him the flexibility to develop a rhythm from machine to machine. Bob says you can produce 20-30% more standing. He estimates a gross income of $63 an hour.

There are many opportunities for production work, depending where you live. Once you begin don't be surprised to find you're in demand. Word spreads, and the work grows.

PART FIVE:

SUMMARY &

INCOME INFO

Summary & Income Information

If you've read this entire book you should have a pretty good idea by now what type of sewing-related business appeals most to you. However, the bottom line is of great importance: it's vital to know if you can make any money in your chosen field. Also, how do you know if you have the skills necessary to succeed? The following checklist of information by area of specialty should help.

EXPLANATION OF THIS SECTION

The possible income shown for each section is based on a **gross figure** – what the customer pays. Be aware, if you have never had a business before, all expenses are paid from this amount. Charging too little, a common mistake made by beginners (and some with experience!), can result in slave wages to the stitcher.

Some expenses to consider, even in a homebased business:

- ◆ Telephone
- ◆ Utilities
- ◆ Rent or mortgage
- ◆ Depreciation (machines, furniture, computer)
- ◆ Fees, licenses
- ◆ Taxes
- ◆ Office supplies
- ◆ Sewing supplies
- ◆ Postage
- ◆ Interest on loans
- ◆ Business checking account charges
- ◆ Advertising
- ◆ Stationery

Check with your accountant for more information on the expenses that might apply to your business.

Part 1   Clothing

DRESSMAKING

Success Keys

- Ability to sew well and quickly
- Patternmaking or pattern altering skills
- Fitting expertise
- Diplomacy and tact
- Self-confidence
- Good taste
- Knowledge of quality fabrics
- Up-to-date on fashion
- Creativity

Income Range

Dressmakers gross anywhere from $2 to $30 per hour, depending on their skill level, area of the country in which they live, level of clientele, and number of employees.

Couture-quality sewing is different, or at least it should be, and a higher gross income is possible, up to about $75 an hour. However, as Kenneth King says, customers at this price level expect certain amenities. Also, the designer's name recognition makes a difference as to whether or not she commands such fees.

ALTERATIONS

Success Keys

- Good to excellent sewing skills.
- The ability to sew quickly and accurately.
- Knowledge of how garments are made.
- Ability to judge fit.

Income Range

$5 to $30 per hour, depending on speed, skill and marketing ability. Income also depends on whether the work is done for a third party (as in a dry cleaning business), from a shop, or from a homebased business. Lower fees are paid to alterationists who don't see the customer or mark the garment. The more service to, and direct contact with the customer, the higher the gross to the service provider.

CUSTOM DESIGN

Success Keys

- Excellent patternmaking skills a must (or the communication skills to advise a patternmaker of your requirements).
- Excellent sewing skills.
- Knowledge of how garments are made.
- A creative mind, capable of envisioning solutions to problems, and/or unusual designs.

Income Range

Similar to dressmaking, above. $7 to $40 per hour.

BRIDAL/FORMALWEAR

Success Keys

- Excellent sewing skills.
- The ability to alter existing patterns, or create your own patterns.
- The patience of Job, for dealing with frantic brides, and the ability to listen to the problems of the brides, ranging from jewelry decisions to seating at the reception.
- The ability to hold up well under extreme pressure.
- A large workspace, for cutting out and sewing long skirts.
- Good sense of design.
- Excellent handsewing skills.

Income range

Similar to Dressmaking, above. $7 to $45 per hour, depending on the quality of the work, location, and reputation of the designer.

TAILORING

Success Keys

- Excellent tailoring skills, including pressing and handsewing.
- Thorough knowledge of fabrics, including the "guts" of tailoring – the interfacings and other aids to shaping.
- Customer service skills; a professional and impersonal, yet sensitive way of dealing with the differences in body styles.
- Good understanding of body complexities, such as how large biceps can change the customer's perceived size.

Income Range

$8 to $40 per hour. Made-to-measure tailoring is different; this specialty equates more with retailing than with sewing as a business, and carries a higher potential for profit.

Part 2   Home Dec Sewing

Success keys

- An eye for color and fabric choices.
- Excellent sewing skills, with particular attention to speed and pattern matching ability.
- Industrial machine for sewing heavy fabrics.
- Large work area.
- Knowledge of trends in home dec.

Income Range

$6 to $35 per hour. Again, this depends on location, designer's skill and experience, and whether or not the customer is buying directly or through a decorator.

Part 3   Paraphernalia

CRAFTS - Overview

Success Keys

- A creative mind.
- The ability to quickly turn out dozens, sometimes hundreds of the same thing.
- Good selling or marketing skills, or an arrangement with an agent.
- Equipment needs depend on the product.

CRAFTS - Overview (continued)

Income Range

Anywhere from a negative to $40/hour. Depends on product mix and desirability, the quality of your work, and the marketing methods employed. Unless your product is unique and timely, your income is only limited to the amount of production and marketing you can accomplish successfully. This depends wholly on the usefulness and salability of your product. Custom items can command a larger dollar than those made assembly line style, but may also take longer to create.

DOLLS & TOYS

Success keys

- Creativity and originality for fresh designs that will sell.
- Willingness to work on small items.
- Medium to excellent sewing skills.
- Knowledge of the latest trends in dolls and toys.
- When sewing period dolls and clothing, attention to detail, especially historic accuracy.

SPORTING EQUIPMENT

Success keys

- Knowledge of the marketplace.
- Knowledge of the sport and the customer for whom the items are designed.
- Good to excellent design skills.
- Originality, and execution of ideas.
- Access to appropriate fabrics.
- Good marketing skills.

EMBROIDERY

Success keys

- Willingness to work with computers.
- Ability to work with mechanicals.
- Willingness to make many of the same item.
- Large workspace for the machines.

BOATS, PLANES & AUTOMOBILES

Success keys

- Knowledge of your market; such specialization requires development of a niche.
- Industrial machines and large working space is a must.
- Ability to sew fast.
- Some of these specialties may require strength, when using heavy canvas, for instance.

HORSE INDUSTRY; LUGGAGE

Success keys

- Knowledge of the industry you're trying to court.
- Proximity to horse stables, for that specialty.
- Access to necessary fabrics and patterns.
- If sewing heavy duty items, industrial machines.
- Excellent sewing skills; fitting skills for clothing; tailoring skills for shadbellies, etc.

QUILTING SERVICES

Success keys:

- Working knowledge of quilt patterns and acceptable heirloom quality.
- Excellent handsewing skills, if hand quilting.
- If machine quilting, good eye/hand coordination.
- An eye for color, and other design abilities.
- Large workspace, if machine quilting.
- Good eyes, period!

Income Range

Depending on how you charge, by the job or by the hour, and how quickly you work. In some areas, quilting is very competitive. Check what others are charging to determine your rates. If you're machine quilting, ask the machine dealer what others are charging.

BANNERS & FLAGS

Success Keys

- Large workspace, including storage for stockpile of fabrics
- Ability to buy fabric wholesale, if mass producing designs.
- Ability and desire to work on same design over and over
- Good color sense
- Factory sewing skills, as opposed to dressmaker skills
- Access to computerized lettering/logo enlargement
- Good marketing and selling skills, or access to an agent.
- In the case of color guard banners, musical knowledge and intro to band directors
- For sacred banners, knowledge of religious symbols and holydays

Income Range

$5 to $30 per hour. Liturgical work is probably on the low end of the scale, while commercial banner work would bring in the most.

Part 4   Other Industry Fields

FABRIC STORE, MAIL ORDER, SEWING MACHINE STORE

Success Keys

- Thorough knowledge of retail math and accounting practices.
- Excellent marketing and selling skills.
- For retail stores, enough capital to carry the store for at least six months.

- Accounting and legal advice will contribute heavily towards success.
- Knowledge of your product is essential!
- Commitment to customer service.

Income Range

These businesses can take several years until they are self-sustaining. Once they have reached this point, though, the amount of income will depend on many things: location, marketing, competition in the area, employees, suppliers, and much more. All things being equal, a sewing machine store can expect to net $35,000 to $50,000 after about three years, and a fabric store has similar potential.

TEACHING, VIDEO PRODUCTION

Success Keys

- Good to excellent communication and "people" skills; the ability to put yourself on the beginner's level.
- Stamina, for long classes involving standing and bending.
- Good understanding of the material being presented.
- Pleasant, clear speaking voice.
- Access to large workspace for hands-on classes, possibly supply of machines for student use.
- For national seminars, an exceptional constitution that can withstand the abuse of travel.
- Not absolutely necessary, but helpful: a sense of humor, especially when teaching children.
- For videos, access to professional quality video equipment or a videographer. (Also, see Mail Order, above.)
- The ability to generate excitement to others; this makes them come back for more!

Income Range

From $5 to $30 an hour for regular sewing and craft classes, to as much as $50 to $100 and up for seminars and lectures. The hourly income goes up once the initial preparation of the lesson plans, handouts, etc. has been taken into consideration. If you are teaching the same class for a long time, that preparation is significantly lessened. In the case of traveling seminars, time spent getting from one place to another, and the disadvantages (or advantages!) of being away from home should also be considered.

WRITING

Success Keys

- Ability to write, combined with solid knowledge of a subject.
- Excellent communication skills.
- A computer is almost essential.
- A publisher, or the willingness to self-publish, and the knowledge to do so.
- If self-publishing, see Retail, above.
- The ability and desire to promote your work, whether self-published, or by traditional means.

Income Range

This varies widely, and depends on the publishing method, your interest and abilities regarding promotion, financial outlay before and after the work is completed, and the salability of the work. I recommend finding all you can about the publishing business first.

PATTERN PUBLICATION

Success Keys

- Excellent pattern drafting skills.
- Access to a printer for reproduction of the finished patterns. (Some companies use blueprint makers.)
- The ability to write clear, easy to understand directions is a must.

Income Range

As above, income varies widely. See Writing.

PIECEWORK, FACTORY SEWING

Success Keys

- The ability to sew quickly and accurately.

- Industrial machines to fit the job.
- Willingness to perform the same job many times.
- Large workspace for some jobs.
- Willingness to work on a deadline, if need be.
- Proximity to industry that needs such service, or contacts elsewhere.
- Access to machine repair locally is vital!

Income Range

Expect to make between $5 to $25 per hour, depending on your skill level and speed. Industrial machines will quickly pay for themselves.

PART SIX:

REFERENCE SECTION

↳ **Associations**

↳ **Resources**

↳ **Periodicals**

PROFESSIONAL ASSOCIATIONS

Professional Sewing Association, Inc. (PSA), C/O Gay Costa, 43 Eswin Street, Cincinnati, OH 45218. (513) 230-5368. Open to anyone who sews for profit. Dues $40/calendar year, individual; $60/year, business membership (allows any two employees to attend meetings). Newsletter subscription $15 Annual *BEYOND PIN MONEY* Conference for Sewing Professionals.

Custom Tailors and Design Association (CTDA), 17 East 45th Street, New York, NY 10017.

Professional Needle Guild, Inc. (PNG), PO Box 40236, Cleveland, OH 44140. (216) 843-4121. Open to anyone who has a sewing business. Monthly meetings, newsletter.

Greater Metro Professional Sewing Association (GMPSA), PO Box 23032, Richfield, MN 55423. This group has a program set up to certify members in various types of sewing specialties: Dressmaking, Alterations, etc. Monthly meetings and monthly newsletter.

Rhode Island Home Sewing Network, C/O Cheryl Lepore, 70 New Gardners Neck Road, Swansea, MA 02777-2524. Open to anyone with an interest in "sewing for personal pleasure or profit". Six meetings a year, annual bus trip to New York City's garment district. Dues run from June to June.

Professional Dressmakers Association, C/O Kim Baumunk-Kleine, Ultimate Stitch, Inc., 5401 Goethe Avenue, St. Louis, MO 63109. (314) 832-8637. Meetings in every month but May and December.

Professional Association of Custom Clothiers (PACC), PO Box 8071, Medford, OR 97504-0071. (503)772-4119. Regional and local chapters; quarterly newsletter with chapter information. Annual conference.

Fashion Group International, Inc., 597 Fifth Avenue, New York, NY 10017. (212) 593-1715. Fashion trend info, bi-monthly newsletter, annual directory. Membership open to anyone connected to the fashion industry. Prospects are sponsored by members in good standing.

The International Costumer's Guild, 1444 Arona Street, St. Paul, MN 55108.

The Greater Columbia Fantasy Costumer's Guild, PO Box 683, Columbia, MD 21045.

National Association of Female Executives (NAFE), 30 Irving Place, 5th Floor, New York, NY 10003. (212) 477-2200. Membership includes monthly magazine, *Female Executive*, annual directory, career and entrepreneurial assistance, and a host of other benefits.

The National Needlework Association (TNNA) (203) 431-8226. Mainly for retailers, but has a category for needlework crafters.

Association of Crafts & Creative Industries (ACCI), 1100-H Brandywine Blvd., PO Box 2188, Zanesville, OH 43702-2188. (614) 452-4541. Nearly 5,000 members worldwide, with categories including retailers, mail-order companies, professional crafters, designers, teachers, consultants and publishers. Annual trade shows.

Hobby Industry Association (HIA)/Mid-Atlantic Craft & Hobby Association (MATCH), 319 East 54th Street, PO Box 348, Elmwood Park, NJ 07407. (201) 794-1133. Categories of membership include designers, retailers, manufacturers, professional craft producers, and others. Joint producers of East Coast Craft Show (ECCS). Quarterly newsletter.

International Sewing Machine Association (ISMA), 1100-H Brandywine Blvd., PO Box 2188, Zanesville, OH 43702-2188. (614) 452-4541. Open to consultants, designers, teachers, retailers, manufacturer, publishers and sewing machine dealers. Annual trade shows. Monthly newspaper.

Window Coverings Association of America (WCAA), 825 So. Waukegan Rd. Suite A8-111, Lake Forest, IL 60045-2665. (708) 480-7955. Though this association is mainly for designers, many designer seamstresses belong.

Decorative Window Coverings Association, 1050 N. Lindbergh Blvd., St. Louis, MO 63132-2994. (314) 991-3470.

Atlantic Window Covering Association, Ross's Corner, RR 3, Summerside, Prince Edward Island, Canada C1N 4J9. (902) 835-9798.

Window Covering Association of British Columbia, 4620 Viking Way, Unit 140, Richmond, BC, Canada V6V 2L5 (604) 276-9680.

American Home Sewing & Craft Association (AHSCA), 1375 Broadway, New York, NY 10018. (212) 302-2150. Membership open to retailers, manufacturers, dealers, consultants, writers and teachers in the "home sewing" market. Annual trade shows. Bi-monthly industry newsletter.

Embroidery Trade Association International, 745 Gilbert Road, Suite 124-201, Gilbert, AZ 85234. (800) 584-7918. For commercial embroidery businesses.

Industrial Fabrics Association International (IFAI), 345 Cedar St., Suite 800, St. Paul, MN 55101-1088. (612) 222-8215. This organization is an incredible resource of industry publications and books, fabric specification information, and resource information for marine, industrial, awning, architecture, and geotechnical fabrics. An industry information hotline is available to members.

Ohio Arts & Crafts Guild, Canton, OH (419) 884-9622. Open to many categories of crafters. Members have access to Visa/MasterCard accounts at preferred rates, conferences, and a newsletter.

American Apparel Manufacturers Association (AAMA). A national trade association, representing apparel manufacturers and suppliers. (800) 520-2262.

Seattle Textile Computer User's Group (STCUG), PO Box 70234, Bellevue, WA 98007. Rich source of information on many textile-related subjects, as they pertain to computing. Bi-monthly newsletter.

American Sewing Guild (ASG), PO Box 8476, Medford, OR 97504-0476. (503) 772-4059. Though this focus of this group is to promote home sewing, there are members with sewing-related businesses.

RESOURCES

Small Business Development Centers. Call your local Chamber of Commerce to find the nearest one.

Service Corps of Retired Executives (SCORE). Call your nearest Small Business Administration office for information.

T.I.P. Resource Guide, T.I.P. (Trends in Progess), Inc. 55 West 39th Street, Suite 708, New York, NY 10018. (212)398-9273. At press time, this annually published guide was $150/year (check or American Express). Included are 1,000 resources for domestic and imported fabrics, with over 250 types listed; 450 trim resources in 90 categories; 160 resources for support materials (linings, boning, shoulder pads); and 170 resources for hand and machine yarns. Also included are industry services listing, and Fabric Market codes, and minimum requirements for each company.

The Crafts Supply Sourcebook, available from bookstores. 2600 listings of mail-order sources.

Beckman's Handcrafted Gift Show, Industry Productions of America, PO Box 27337, Los Angeles, CA 90027. (213) 962-5424.

Fairchild Books and Visuals, 7 West 34th Street, New York, NY 10001. (212) 630-3880. Publishes a variety of titles regarding sewing, pattern drafting, draping, and business.

Textile Reproductions, Kathleen B. Smith, Box 48, West Chesterfield, MA 01084. (413) 296-4437. Catalogue of materials and supplies for historic textile arts and reproductions.

Quilt Market, 14520 Memorial Dr. #54, Houston, TX 77079. (713) 496-6864. Trade show with a quilting, textile and craft focus. World's largest international quilt show.

Entrepreneur Magazine's Small Business Expo. (800) 864-6864. Produces trade shows in various regions of the US for small businessowners.

Sewn Products Expo. Epic Enterprises, 8989 Rio San Diego Dr., #160, San Diego, CA 92108. (800) 599-9752. Production equipment, supplies and services used in the manufacturing of apparel and non-apparel sewn products in the US and Mexico.

Bobbin Show. Produced by Bobbin Blenheim, PO Box 1986, Columbia, SC 29202. One of the top 200 industry trade shows in terms of size, this show attracts manufacturers and sewn products suppliers. Best for those looking for finished products or large equipment needs.

Great Lakes Textile Show, PO Box 450670, Westlake, OH 44145. (216) 871-3600. Regional wholesale show for fabric and trims, exhibiting in Toledo three times a year.

Coomers Craft Mall, 6012 Reef Point Lane, Suite F, Ft. Worth, TX 76135. (817) 237-4588. Locations in seven states. Has a Remote Stocking Program that allows professional crafters to ship products to any Coomers location

The Unicorn Textile Book Catalog, Unicorn Books and Crafts, Inc., 1338 Ross St., Petaluma, CA 94954-6502. (800) 289-9276. Large resource for many types of textile-related books. Great newspaper style catalogue.

Schools:

Cheryl Strickland's Professional Drapery Workroom School, PO Box 867, Swannanoa, NC 28778. (800) 222-1415.

Bridal Sewing School, 4600 Briedenbaugh Lane, Glenarm, MD 21057. (410) 592-5711. Periodic week-long classes in sewing bridal gowns.

University of Rhode Island Cooperative Extension, Woodward Hall, Kingston, RI 02881-0804. (401) 762-0960. Offers a two-year Master Seamstress Certificate Program.

Palmer/Pletsch Associates, PO Box 12046, Portland, OR 97212-0046. (503) 274-0687. Classes in teaching, pants fitting and more.

Teaching Systems:

Cheri Sizemore, Cheri's Sewing Academy, 3529 Chaffin Dr., Ft. Worth, TX 76118. (817) 284-0970.

Primary Patterns, 16745 Edinborough, Detroit, MI 48219. (313) 538-4201. Children's patterns and teaching system.

Stretch & Sew, Inc., 3895 East 19th, PO Box 185, Eugene, OR 97440. (503) 726-9000. Lesson plans for teaching many subjects.

Videos:

SewPro Workshop, 2315-B Forest Dr., Suite 50, Annapolis, MD 21401. (800) 355-1137. Mary Ellen Flury's tailoring videos.

Islander School of Fashion Arts, Inc., PO Box 66, Grants Pass, OR 97526. (503) 479-3906.

T&M Creations, (800) 767-9229. Slipcovering and drapery videos.

While these two companies are primarily known for their retail catalogues, they both also sell wholesale to retailers, and may offer discounts to educators and/or small businesses:

Nancy's Notions, Ltd., PO Box 683, Beaver Dam, WI 53916-0683. (414) 887-0391.

Clotilde, Inc., 2 Sew Smart Way, Stevens Point, WI 54481-8031. (715) 341-2824.

Patternmaking Software:

Dress Shop 2.0. Livingsoft, Inc., PO Box 1030, Janesville, CA 96114-1030. (800) 626-1262.

Fittingly Sew ™, Bartley Software, Inc., 72 Robertson Rd., Box 26122, Nepean, Ontario, Canada K2H 9R6. (800) 661-5209.

Personal Patterns 2.0 *and*

Personal Patterns Jackets, Water Fountain Software, 13 E. 17th Street, 3rd Floor, New York, NY 10003. (212) 929-6204.

Author's Note: Reviews of each of the above pattern drafting systems appeared in *Sew Up A Storm: The Newsletter for the Sewing Entrepreneur.* For reprints, send $2.50 for each to: SewStorm Publishing, 944 Sutton Road, Cincinnati, OH 45230-3581. Be sure to state which reprints you would like.

Cadterns, 1500 Merklin St. #104, White Rock, BC, Canada V4B 4C5 (604) 536-5199.

OptiKAD, Cad Cut, Inc., Three Mile Bridge Road, PO Box 856, Montpelier, VT 05602. (800) 588-4055. A professional grading system for garment production.

Patternmaking System:

"Cut To The Fit", by Karen K. Howland. Kensinger Press, 9557 Creekside, Loveland, OH 45140. A hand-drafting system that works. At this writing this book had not yet been priced, so write for ordering information. Classes also available.

Home Dec patterns:

M'Fay, PO Box 471187, Charlotte, NC 28247. (704) 847-1464.

Patterns Plus, PO Box 50428, Ft. Myers, FL 33905-0428. (813) 543-2355.

Workroom consultant:

Kitty Stein, Workroom Concepts, PO Box 283, Clearbrook, VA 22624. (703) 667-5939. Also sells forms for drapery workrooms.

Horse-related patterns:

SuitAbility, 848 S. Myrtle Avenue, Suite 5, Monrovia, CA 91016-3455. (818) 303-1649.

Jean Hardy Patterns, 2152 LaCuesta Dr., Santa Ana, CA 92705.

Skating patterns:

Murielle Roy & Co., Dept. 1, 67 Platts Mill Road, Naugatuck, CT 06770. (203) 729-0480.

Special Needs Clothing Patterns:

Tu-Rights, Doris Gathright, 2704 E. Poplar Ave., Victoria, TX 77901. (512) 573-4825.

Elizabeth Lee Designs, Box 696, Bluebell, UT 84007. Maternity and postpartum nursing patterns.

Lingerie Patterns & supplies:

Kieffer's, PO Box 7500, Jersey City, NJ 07307. (201) 798-2266.

Sew Sassy Lingerie, 7500 S. Memorial Pky., Suite 133, Huntsville, AL 35802. (205) 883-1209.

Specialties, 4425 Cotton Hanlon Rd., Montour Falls, NY 14865. (607) 594-2021.

Elan Pattern Co., 534 Sandalwood Dr., El Cajon, CA 92021.

Suppliers of outdoor fabrics, patterns & supplies:

The Rainshed, 707 NW 11th Street, Corvallis, OR 97330. (503) 753-8900.

Green Pepper, 3918 West 1st, Eugene, OR 97402. (503) 345-6665.

Frostline Kits, 2525 River Road, Grand Junction, CO 81505. (800) KITS-USA.

Sunshine Foam Rubber & Upholstery Supply Co., 1103 Alfred St., Cincinnati, OH 45214. (513) 681-7300. (Suppliers of many grades of foam, automotive supplies, much more.)

Costume patterns & supplies:

Amazon Drygoods, 2218 East 11th Street, Davenport, IA 52803-3760. (319) 322-6800.

Raiments, PLO Box 93095, Pasadena, CA 91109. (818) 797-2723.

Jehlor Fantasy Fabrics, 730 Andover Park West, Seattle, WA 98188. (206) 575-8250.

Harper House, PO Box 39, Williamstown, PA 17098. (717) 647-7807.

Folkwear Patterns, C/O The Taunton Press, PO Box 5506, Newtown, CT 06470-5506.

Fall Creek Sutlery, PO Box 530, Freedom, CA 95019. (408) 728-1888.

NE Shutsa Traders, PO Box 186, Haven, KS 67542. (316) 465-3359.

Campbell's Designs, Box 400, Gratz, PA 17030-0400.

Old World Enterprises, Dept. 302, 29036 Kepler Ct., Cold Spring, MN 56320.

The Whole Costumer's Catalogue, Box 207, Main Street, Beallsville, PA 15313. (412) 632-3242. Source reference for costumers.

Dance Fantasy, PO Box 3249, Hollywood, CA 91609. Ethnic dance costume information; also dance instruction and more.

Labels:

Blond Woven Label Co., 7516 Arden Road, Cabin John, MO 20818. (301) 229-8993.

Sterling Name Tape Company, PO Box 939, Winsted, CT 06098. (203) 379-5142.

Name Maker, Inc., PO Box 43821, Atlanta, GA 30378. (800) 241-2890.

Northwest Tag & Label, 110 Foothills Road, Lake Oswego, OR 97034.

General Label Mfg., PO Box 640371, Miami, FL 33164. (800) 944-4696.

Heirloom Woven Labels, PO Box 428, Moorestown, NJ 08057. (609) 722-1618.

Covered buttons:

Fashion Touches, PO Box 804, Bridgeport, CT 06604.

Supplies, including professional pressing equipment:

Banasch's, 2810 Highland Avenue, Cincinnati, OH 45212. (800) 543-0355. (Also sells industrial sewing machines.)

Ely E. Yawitz Co., 1717 Olive St., PO Box 14325, St. Louis, MO 63178-4325. (800) 325-7915.

B&G Lieberman, 2420 Distribution St., Charlotte, NC 28203. (800) 438-0346. (Also sells industrial machines.)

Brewer Sewing Supplies, 3800 W. 42nd St., Chicago, IL 60632. (800) 444-3111.

Greenberg & Hammer, Inc., 24 W. 57th Street, New York, NY 10019-3918. (800) 955-5135.

Baer Fabrics, 515 E. Market St., Louisville, KY 40202.

National Thread & Supply Corp., 695 Red Oak Road, Stockbridge, GA 30281. (800) 331-7600.

Sewing & Craft Supply (SCS), 9631 NE Colfax, Portland, OR 97220-1232. (800) 542-8025. (Also sells OmniStitch machines.)

SouthStar Supply Co., PO Box 90147, Nashville, TN 37209. (800) 288-6739. (Also sells industrial machines.) This catalogue company caters to manufacturers. Carries KOGOS Apparel Books: many "how-to" volumes on manufacturing topics, including foreign language.

Sewing Emporium, 1079 Third Avenue, Chula Vista, CA 92010. (619) 420-3490. (Specializes in parts for machines. Sells some machines.)

Washington Millinery Supply Inc., PO Box 5718, Derwood, MD 20855. (301) 963-4444. (Bridal supplies)

Machines:

All Brand Discount Sew & Serg Co., 9789 Florida Blvd., Baton Rouge, LA 70815. (800) 739-7374. (The "yellow ad" in consumer sewing magazines. Sells industrial machines, also.)

MIM/Parts Plus, 1110 Airport Parkway, SW, Gainesville, GA 30501. (800) 441-2716.

Banasch's, above.

Archie Johnson & Sons, 2323 Lake Wheeler Rd., Raleigh, NC 27603. (919) 833-2791. Inventor of the Johnson Ruffling Machine.

Embroidery:

Meistergram, 3517 W. Wenover Avenue, Greensboro, NC 27407. (800) 321-0486.

Melco, 1575 W. 124th Avenue, Denver, CO 80234. (800) 366-3526. (Also make chenille machines.)

SCS, above. OmniStitch machines.

Pantograms Mfg. Co., 6807 S. MacDill Ave., Tampa, FL 33611. (800) 872-1555.

Gunold & Stickma, (800) 62-BEST-1. Large, commercial quality machines.

Quilting machines:

Gammill Quilting Machine Co., 1452 W. Gibson, West Plains, MO 65775. (800) 659-8224.

Nolting's Longarm Manufacturing, Inc., Rt. 3, Box 147, Hwy. 52 E., Stover, MO 65078-9420. (314) 377-2713.

Kenquilt Mfg. Co., 113 Pattie St., Wichita, KS 67211. (316) 262-3438.

American Professional Quilting Supplies, Hwy. 30 East, Carroll, IA 51401. (712) 792-5820.

Consumer Shows:

In Stitches/Make it Myself, In Stitches Consulting, Ltd., 936 Peace Portal Dr., PO Box 8014-#42, Blaine, WA 98231-8014. (604) 538-7444. (800) 468-6739 for brochures.

Original Sewing & Crafts Expo, 26612 Center Ridge Road, Westlake, OH 44145. (216) 899-4712.

American Stitches, 1385 Clyde Road, Highland, MI 48357. (810) 889-3111.

Creative Sewing & Needleart Expositions. (800) 325-1882.

Creative Sewing and Needlework Festival, International Showcase Associates, Inc. 2900 John St., Suite 200, Markham, Ontario L3R 5G3 Canada. (800) 291-2030.

PERIODICALS

Sew Up A Storm: The Newsletter for Sewing Entrepreneurs, SewStorm Publishing, 944 Sutton Road, Cincinnati, OH 45230-3581. Quarterly newsletter, focus on business. No "how to sew", no advertising. 12 pages, $25 per year, US funds($32, Canada; $38, International).

The "Business" of Sewing. Collins Publications, 3233 Grand Avenue, Suite N-294, Chino Hills, CA 91709. (800) 795-8999. Quarterly newsletter, focus on sewing as a business.

Sew What? The International Newsletter for Professional Drapery Workrooms. Cheryl Strickland, 101 Strickland Terrace, Swannanoa, NC 28778. (800) 222-1415. Monthly newsletter; workroom school.

Drapery & Window Coverings Magazine. Clark Publishing, PO Box 13079, North Palm Beach, FL 33408-7079. (800) 833-9056. Monthly magazine.

Window Fashions Magazine, 4225 White Bear Pkwy. Suite 400, St. Paul, MN 55110. (612) 293-1544. Sponsors trade shows; compiling directory of workrooms.

Seamstress Network, LaVelle Pinder, 9102 Collingwood, Austin, TX 78748. (512) 282-0717. Quarterly window covering newsletter; workroom school.

National Home Business Report, Barbara Brabec Productions, PO Box 2137, Naperville, IL 60567. Quarterly mini-magazine for homebased business owners.

The Crafts Report: The Business Journal for the Crafts Industry, 300 Water Street, PO Box 1992, Wilmington, DE 19899. (302) 656-2209, (800) 777-7098. Monthly tabloid.

Crafting for Profit. Meredith Corporation, 1912 Grand Ave., Des Moines, IA 50309-3379. Monthly newsletter, focus on the nuts and bolts of producing and selling crafts.

Stitches Magazine, The Magazine for the Commercial Embroidery Industry. Intertec Publishing, 9800 Metcalf, Overland Park, KS 66212-2215. (913) 341-1300. Semi-monthly magazine.

Embroidery Business News. (602) 990-1101.

Embroidery/Monogram Business. (214) 239-3060.

Home Business Journal, 2536 E. Impala Avenue, Mesa, AZ 85204. (602) 892-6221. Bi-monthly.

Made-To-Measure Magazine, Halpert Publishing House, 600 Central Avenue, Highland Park, IL 60035. For the tailoring industry.

The National Clothesline, BPS Communications, PO Box 516, Pottstown, PA 19464-0516. For the dry cleaning industry, but includes textile news.

Craftrends/SewBusiness, PJS Publications, 2 News Plaza, Box 1790, Peoria, IL 61656. Published monthly; mainly for craft retailers, fabric stores, and professional crafters. A short section on sewing is included in each issue.

Profitable Craft Merchandising (PCM), PJS Publications, 2 News Plaza, Box 1790, Peoria, IL 61656. (309) 682-6626. Published monthly; primarily for craft retailers and suppliers, professional crafters.

Horse & Rider, 1060 Calle Cordillera, Suite 103, San Clemente, CA 92673.

The Creative Machine, Open Chain Publishing, Inc., PO Box 2634-NL, Menlo Park, CA 94026-2634. (415) 366-4440. Quarterly consumer newsletter. No advertising, reviews of patterns, books, machines, and other sewing-related merchandise.

Threads, The Taunton Press, PO Box 5506, Newtown, CT 06470-5506. (800) 283-7252. Bi-monthly consumer sewing publication.

Sew News, PJS Publications, #2 News Plaza, PO Box 1790, Peoria, IL 61656-1790. (800) 289-6397. Monthly consumer sewing publication.

Vogue Patterns, 161 Avenue of the Americas, New York, NY 10013. Bi-monthly consumer sewing publication.

PART SEVEN:

BIBLIOGRAPHY

SEW TO SUCCESS, Kathleen Spike, Palmer/Pletsch Associates, 1990. Described as an autobiography of Spike's experiences as a custom dressmaker. Offers advice on how to emulate her success. Also includes four short profiles of other sewing professionals in Chapter 3.

THE "BUSINESS" OF SEWING, Barbara Wright Sykes, Collins Publications, 1992. Another "how-to" for sewing professionals; mainly stresses the mechanics of maintaining a custom sewing business. Page 25 lists eight specialties in custom sewing but does not elaborate. Chapter 9 is a brief discussion of teaching and writing as opportunities for profit.

SEWING AS A HOME BUSINESS, Mary A. Roehr, 1984. Focuses on details of starting a sewing business and the day-to-day operations. Listing of specialty choices appears on pages 11 and 12.

SEWING AS A BUSINESS, Beth Duncan, Mississippi Cooperative Extension Service, in cooperation with the American Home Sewing & Crafts Association. Publication 1667. Legal, financial, marketing, pricing and customer relations advice for start-up sewing businesses.

PRICE IT RIGHT, Claire Shaeffer, PO Box 157, Palm Springs, CA 92263. 1984. Outlines a system of pricing alterations, without tying it to a particular dollar amount. Any monetary unit can be used, and prices can be changed easily to reflect inflation.

UNIT PRICING FOR DRESSMAKING, Karen K. Howland. Kensinger Press, 9557 Creekside Dr., Loveland, OH 45140. 1994. A system of pricing for dressmaking that gives the dressmaker (and other sewing professionals) a way to charge for the time it takes, rather than how much the customer wants to spend.

YOU CAN MAKE MONEY FROM YOUR ARTS AND CRAFTS, Steve and Cindy Long, Mark Publishing, 1988. While this book mentions few sewn crafts, it is a well-written, complete manual for mass-producing, pricing, marketing and selling hand-crafted products of any kind.

WORKING FROM HOME, Paul and Sarah Edwards, Jeffrey P. Tarcher, Inc., 1990. A comprehensive reference for home-based businesses. Does not mention sewing businesses at all, except in the appendix, which lists more than six pages of possible specialties.

START, RUN & PROFIT FROM YOUR OWN HOME-BASED BUSINESS, Gregory Kishel and Patricia Kishel, John Wiley & Sons, Inc., 1984, 1991. Another reference for working from home, with less depth than the Edwards' book. Has some references to sewing, writing.

SMALL-TIME OPERATOR, Bernard Kamoroff, CPA. Bell Springs, 1993. A guide to starting a business, written by a certified public accountant. Yearly updates are available from the author.

WORKROOM DESIGN: SPACE SOLUTIONS FOR SEWING WORKROOMS, Karen L. Maslowski, SewStorm Publishing, 944 Sutton Road, Cincinnati, OH 45230-3581. 1994. A 24-page guide to setting up your professional workroom, with measurements, lighting hints, and sample floor plans.

101 BEST BUSINESSES TO START, Sharon Kahn

THE NEW ENTREPRENEURS: Women Working From Home, Terri P. Tepper and Nona Dawe Tepper, Universe Books, 1980. Case studies of 40 women who operate home businesses. Personal narratives of a variety of career choices, some of which are sewing-related, characterize this book.

CASH, CASH, WHO'S GOT THE CASH?, Robert Link. The Four Corners Press, Box 7468, Grand Rapids, MI 49510. How to find financing for businesses.

MARKETING WITHOUT MONEY, Nicholas E. Bade, 5966 Halle Farm Dr., Willoughby, OH 44094-3076.

Marketing & Promotion from A to Z, Kay Pegram. Kaymar books, PO Box 5944. Playa del Rey, CA 90296.

DISCOVER DRESSMAKING AS A PROFESSIONAL CAREER, James C. Leiter, Jr. and Joan Stanley, Leiters Designer Fabrics, 1982. Discussion of setting up and succeeding in a dressmaking business. Describes five areas of specialization of dressmaking.

PATTERNS FOR THEATRICAL COSTUME, Katherine Strand Holkeboer. Drama Book Publishers, 1984.

COSTUME DESIGNER'S HANDBOOK, Rosemary Ingham and Liz Covey. Heinemann Educational Books, 1992. A comprehensive, amply illustrated, guide to the nuts and bolts of designing costumes for the stage. Includes a 28-page annotated bibliography, and another 26 pages of resources.

COSTUME DESIGN, Lynn Pecktal. Back Stage Books, 1993.

THE COSTUMEMAKER'S ART, Thom Boswell. Lark Books, 1992.

SLIPCOVERS & BEDSPREADS, Sunset Books, Lane Publishing, 1979.

CURTAINS, DRAPERIES & SHADES, Sunset Books, Lane Publishing, 1979.

HOW TO MAKE PILLOWS, Sunset Books, Lane Publishing, 1980.

UPHOLSTERY, DRAPES and SLIP COVERS, HOW TO MAKE and REPAIR THEM YOURSELF, Dorothy Wagner, Wm. H. Wise & Co., Inc., 1955.

THE COMPLETE BOOK OF SOFT FURNISHINGS, Ward Lock Limited, 1986.

SEWING FOR THE HOME, Singer Sewing Reference Library, Cy DeCosse Incorporated, 1984.

MORE SEWING FOR THE HOME, Singer Sewing Reference Library, Cy DeCosse Incorporated, 1987.

SEWING PROJECTS FOR THE HOME, Singer Sewing Reference Library, Cy DeCosse Incorporated, 1991.

CREATIVE SERGING FOR THE HOME, Lynette Ranney Black and Linda Wisner, Palmer/Pletsch Incorporated, 1991.

LAURA ASHLEY BOOK OF HOME DECORATING, Edited by Charyn Jones, Harmony Books, 1989.

BANNERS: Extra Ordinary Banners for Ordinary Times, George Collopy. Resource Publishing, 1992. Liturgical banner how-tos.

THE BANNER BOOK, Betty Wolfe. Morehouse Publishing. Spiralbound manual on church banner construction.

HOW TO DESIGN AND MAKE BANNERS, Gisela Banbury and Angela Dewar. Morehouse Publishing, 1992. A primer for those interested in making church banners. Designs included.

BANNERS WITH PIZZAZZ, Diane Guelzow. Resource Publishing, 1992. Patterns and sewing information on banners for home use.

SOFT KITES AND WINDSOCKS, Jim Rowlands. St. Martins Press, 1992.

SEWING CHURCH LINENS, Elizabeth Joseph. Morehouse Publishing. Includes diagrams and useful information for hemming cloths, choosing linens, and many liturgical patterns.

EMBROIDERY IN THE CHURCH, Dorothea Hall. Morehouse Publishing. Expand your access to patterns with this book.

CHURCH EMBROIDERY, Beryl Dean. Morehouse Publishing. Construction and decoration of church vestments and ecclesiastical furnishings.

GOLD AND SILVER EMBROIDERY, Kit Pyman, Editor. Morehouse Publishing. Color illustrations of combining appliqué with goldwork, tambour and hand beading, machine embroidery, lettering, and other techniques.

HOME-BASED MAIL ORDER, William J. Bond. 1990. McGraw-Hill, Inc. Everything you need to know to start a home mail order business.

PHOTOGRAPHING YOUR CRAFTWORK, Steve Meltzer.

NON-CREDIT INSTRUCTION, Lea Leavers Oldham. 1994. Info-Tec, Inc., PO Box 40092, Cleveland, OH 44140. Teaching tips.

Potterton Books, The Old Rectory, Sessay, Thirsk, North Yorkshire, Yo7 3LZ, England. International Phone: +44 1845 501218. This company offers catalogue of all sorts of home dec books, many published in the United Kingdom.

Index

–I–

–J–

–K–

–T–

SEW UP A STORM: The Newsletter for Sewing Entrepreneurs

This **12-page**, information-packed quarterly newsletter includes information in every issue about the following:

- Marketing
- Book & Product Reviews
- Customer Relations
- Business Tax information
- Resources
- Professional Associations
- Computer News
- Calendar of Events
- Industrial Machines

Articles are written by both industry insiders and business owners in various sewing-related fields.

Subscribe today, don't miss a single issue!

Rates: 4 issues for $20, US; $28, Canadian; $35, International.

Sew Up A Storm: All the Way to the Bank!
by Karen L. Maslowski

Get your copy of this new book by the editor of *Sew Up A Storm* today! Profiles nearly 100 sewing business owners, with their tips on how to succeed in a sewing-related business. Potential earnings info, pitfalls to avoid, and much, much more included.

Large resource section is worth the price of the book.

220 pages, $19.95, US; $28, Canada; $35, all other.

Workroom Design: Space Solutions for Sewing Workrooms
by Karen L. Maslowski

If you've ever wondered how you can rearrange your workspace more efficiently, this is the book for you! With helpful tips on planning, measuring and storage, you'll learn to maximize the space you have. Also, find out how to improve lighting, select the best flooring, and work more comfortably.

24 pages, $5, US; $7, Canada; $10, all other.

ORDER FORM

YES! Please send me:

_____ ***Sew Up A Storm Newsletter,*** 1 year subscription $20, U.S.; $28, Canada; $35, International (No tax applicable)

_____ ***Sew Up A Storm: All the Way to the Bank!*** $19.95, U.S.; $28, Canadian; $35, International (Add $4.50 shipping for each book)

_____ ***Workroom Design: Space Solutions for Sewing Workrooms,*** $5.00, U.S., $7.00, Canada; $10.00, International (Add $2.00 shipping for each book)

_____ Ohio residents, please add 5 1/2% sales tax for each book only.

_____ Total enclosed (U.S. funds, please)

Please print:

Name _____

Address _____

City _____ State _____

Postal Code _____

Country _____

Phone # (_____) _____

Send orders to and make checks payable to:

Karen Maslowski
C/O SewStorm Publishing
944 Sutton Road
Cincinnati, OH 45230-3581

Photocopies of this form are acceptable

ORDER FORM

YES! Please send me:

____ **_Sew Up A Storm Newsletter,_** 1 year subscription $20, U.S.; $28, Canada; $35, International (No tax applicable)

____ **_Sew Up A Storm: All the Way to the Bank!_** $19.95, U.S.; $28, Canadian; $35, International (Add $4.50 shipping for each book)

____ **_Workroom Design: Space Solutions for Sewing Workrooms,_** $5.00, U.S., $7.00, Canada; $10.00, International (Add $2.00 shipping for each book)

____ Ohio residents, please add 5 1/2% sales tax for each book only.

____ **Total enclosed (U.S. funds, please)**

Please print:

Name _____

Address _____

City _____ State_____

Postal Code _____

Country _____

Phone # (_____) _____

Send orders to and make checks payable to:

Karen Maslowski
C/O SewStorm Publishing
944 Sutton Road
Cincinnati, OH 45230-3581

Photocopies of this form are acceptable